# Danton's Death

# Chandler Editions in Drama

## ROBERT W. CORRIGAN, *Editor*

**Oedipus the King**
by Sophocles
translated by Kenneth Cavander
with an introduction by
Tom F. Driver

**Hippolytus**
by Euripides
translated by Kenneth Cavander
with an introduction by
Robert W. Corrigan

**Lysistrata**
by Aristophanes
translated and with an introduction by Donald Sutherland

**Edward II**
by Christopher Marlowe
with an introduction by
Irving Ribner

**Volpone**
by Ben Jonson
with an introduction by
Henry Lee

**The White Devil**
by John Webster
with an introduction by
Travis Bogard

**Phaedra**
by Jean Racine
translated by Wesley Goddard
with an introduction by
Robert J. Nelson

**The Country Wife**
by William Wycherley
with an introduction by
Steven H. Rubin

**The School for Scandal**
by Richard Brinsley Sheridan
with an introduction by
William L. Sharp

**Danton's Death**
by Georg Buechner
translated and adapted by
James Maxwell
with an introduction by
Theodore C. Hoffman

**Camille and Perdican**
by Alfred de Musset
translated by Peter Meyer
with an introduction by
Leonard C. Pronko

**Rosmersholm**
by Henrik Ibsen
translated by Ann Jellicoe
with an introduction by
Alrik Gustafson

**Miss Julie**
by August Strindberg
translated and with an introduction
by E. M. Sprinchorn

**The Importance of Being Earnest**
by Oscar Wilde
with an introduction by
Henry Popkin

**Crime on Goat Island**
by Ugo Betti
translated by Henry Reed
with an introduction by
G. H. McWilliam

# ❧ ❧ ❧ Danton's Death
# Death GEORG BUECHNER

TRANSLATED AND ADAPTED BY
## James Maxwell

WITH AN INTRODUCTION BY
## Theodore Hoffman

SAN FRANCISCO

CHANDLER PUBLISHING COMPANY

Application to perform *Danton's Death* by Georg Buechner translated and adapted by James Maxwell should be made to The 59 Theatre Company, 3, Soho Square, London, W. 1, England. No performance may take place unless a license has been granted.

# CONTENTS

# INTRODUCTION

*Danton's Death* is often cited as the best first play ever written. It is certainly the best ever written by an undergraduate. Georg Buechner was an extraordinary undergraduate to be sure, and the 1830's produced extraordinary young men. At 21, Buechner was already a disillusioned revolutionary, rusticated from a provincial university to an even more provincial German town by a liberal but suspicious father who was determined that his brilliant biologist son should keep out of trouble and become a doctor like himself. There, in Darmstadt, Buechner, who had previously written only a few radical tracts, set out to write in secret an incredibly unique play which he hoped would provide enough money to escape the country before he was clamped in jail and allowed to molder to death like his friends. The sequel is absurd and romantic. A publisher accepted the play, but the police arrived before the royalty check. Buechner ducked out a back window, escaped to Strasbourg, and in less than two years completed his studies, wrote three more plays (one of which, possibly his best, was burned afterwards by his fiancée as immoral), became a highly regarded university lecturer in comparative anatomy and philosophy, and died of typhus at twenty-three, ministered to by an adoring sentimentalist who recorded his death in a ghoulish diary, including famous last words: "We're dead, dust, ashes; then why are we so anxious to complain?"

As a grand, if delayed, finale, his works died with him, to be revived nearly fifty years afterwards and revered a century later—*Danton's Death* spectacularly staged by Reinhardt, *Woyzeck* turned into one of the great modern operas by Alban Berg. Since his death, Buechner's impact has been acknowledged by every great German playwright: Hebbel, Hauptmann, Wedekind, Brecht. It is in his image, not that of Goethe or Schiller or Wagner, that the best German drama has cast itself. If one likes to investigate trends, Buechner can be studied as a legitimate forerunner of naturalism, social realism, psychological irrationalism, expressionism, and even existential drama. In the search for the taproot of modern drama, there is good reason to dig no further than Georg Buechner.

And as an illuminating postscript, note well that the other two worthwhile German playwrights of the early nineteenth century also died young, frustrated, and unknown: Heinrich von Kleist (1777-1811) of suicide; Christian Grabbe (1801-1836) of dissipation and despair.

What is most immediately impressive, and distracting, about *Danton's Death* is its complexity and multiplicity, even its duplicity. It is not easily dismissed as the erratic vitality of a new playwright trying to do too many things at once, yielding to too many influences, catching too many ideas by the tail. This play has a grand design. For all its fits and starts, it moves relentlessly. Its ideas realize themselves explosively. And its maker juggles his creations with the adroitness of all great artists who know they are in on a cosmic joke. Buechner belongs to that order of playwrights who must violate tradition because they are spurred by revelation and thought which the inherited theatrical forms cannot accommodate, and who produce from unexpected sources shocking new modes of drama. Buechner, as such, is directly in the line of the great playwrights who resist generic classification: Euripides, the author of *The Second Shepherd's Play,* Shakespeare, Molière, Strindberg, Chekhov, Shaw, Brecht. He is perfectly symptomatic of the seemingly inchoate movement which is shaking our theatre today through the plays of Beckett, Genet, Ionesco, Adamov, and Ghelderode. All such playwrights at first appear incoherent, primitive, coarse, confused, undisciplined; and prove upon examination to be motivated by an instinctively organized large view of life, the dynamics of which are far deeper and more complex than the corresponding view of the traditionalists they displace.

For evidence, look no further than Part One, Scene 2 of *Danton's Death,* which juggles dramatic styles with the same frivolous but mordant irony that always characterizes "untheatre." The initial conversation is ostensibly about love, and conveys the requisite wit and bawdry of a comedy of manners. Love and life are set up as the same sort of deadly game, both governed by the copulative principle, but full of chance and deceit, understood fully only through violence. "Know each other?" asks Danton of his wife. "We would have to break our skulls open and tear the thoughts from our brain cells." With the entrance of Camille Desmoulins and Phillippeau, fresh from the opening executions of Robespierre's Reign of Terror, history takes over. The sexual wit turns into mockery of neoclassical sentiments, the comedy of manners into a Scribean heroic drama of intrigue. The deadly game is transferred to the field of politics, but the political ideas, instead of shaping themselves into the dialectal pattern of opposing principles which we expect from historical drama, erupt with a frenzy that suggests a mad struggle between primitive forces far deeper than the ideologies of the age. Camille links "our beloved sinner, France" with "naked gods, orgies . . . loose and luscious love . . . the beautiful buttocks of Venus," and Robespierre's Jacobins with prudery, vegetarianism, gladiators, "throwing to the lions."

Instead of sticking to Schiller's symmetric exposition, Buechner gives us Shakespearean extrapolation. The scene suddenly surges with meaningfulness and seems set up for the consummate great speech. But Buechner then prevents his hero from rising to the bait. In response to Camille's invitation to lead in the battle for Freedom by openly fighting Robespierre, Danton offers only deflating colloquial prose and common-sense sociology. The realities of life are such, he says, that high ideals do not produce commensurate results and he proceeds to taunt his friends with Biblical irony: "I'll make you a prophecy: The statue of Freedom is not yet moulded, but the furnace is lit. All of us might still get our fingers burnt." When asked, ". . . why did you fight for the people in the first place?" he answers that the Jacobins "drove me mad . . . I was itching to kick somebody. It's my nature." The scene ends on a down note, as if all the emotion, idealism, and intelligence displayed did not add up to the real things of life, as if the true battles were being fought somewhere else. The game image suddenly returns as Hérault remarks that Danton will fight Robespierre because "He'll need a pastime. But something livelier than playing cards," leaving us suddenly with a penetrating character sketch, rounding out a scene which has moved with the aimless but definitive direction of Chekhovian naturalism and the ominous mood of psychological melodrama.

Now, identifying the presence of comedy of manners, heroic drama, historical romance, environmental naturalism, and psychological melodrama in one scene out of twenty-one might suggest either pedantry on the critic's part or indecision on the playwright's. But *Danton's Death* is really a play in which form follows content. For Buechner, the French Revolution provided more drama than conventional drama did. It was life, and if the quality of the life it evoked suggested intrigue, romance, raw existence, and unnerving suspense, all wrapped up in one, so be it! *Danton's Death* is a play about Danton's death, and it sets out to convey the order and nature of the events that define that death.

Its playwrighting technique is that of historiography—the methodology, or art if you will, of recreating history. So we get portraits of the principal personages, their beliefs, their actions, and a constant concern with what makes them tick. We get sketches of the salient historic events, exposés of the underlying environmental forces at work, glimpses of unhistorical persons shaped by those forces, and finally we get a permeating image of what this segment of human experience suggests that Life itself is really like.

## II

It is easy to trace Buechner's debt to his predecessors and contemporaries. He can be attached to the "Young Germany" movement, since he was a disillusioned but rebellious realist. On the other hand, his episodic ranging, his broad character sketching, nervous tone, and interest in giving life to the past derive from the *Sturm und Drang* (Storm and Stress) writers who sought to get at the heart of nature by showing vital but anguished individuals caught in a struggle against the choking restrictions of society which leads them either to yield to their natural instincts or to misunderstand life and come a tragic cropper either way.

The early plays of Goethe evolve from the *Sturm und Drang* mood, and the rapidly shifting structure of *Danton's Death* bears a resemblance to *Goetz von Berlichingen*. Certain scenes seem to be inspired directly by *Faust I* (Scene 7 by the "Before the Gate" scene; Scene 9, by the "Forest and Cavern" scene), as does indeed the philosophic introspection of various characters. The play also suggests the shifting tone and narrative ellipsis of the ballads and folk songs which Buechner, like many of his contemporaries, respected. (Witness also his use of the baroque mock hymn which colors the final scene: "Death is God's reaper.") One can wonder if Buechner was among the few early nineteenth-century students of French poetry who knew the works of François Villon, to whose thought Danton's most personal confessions at times bear a curious resemblance, particularly his address to his body (Scene 19), through their testament of mixed defiance and remorse, lassitude and lust, their struggle against the feeling of *accidie*.

However, the playwright who most clearly commands Buechner's respect is Shakespeare, the Shakespeare of the romantic revival, so beloved by the *Sturm und Drangers*—burgeoning with raw, intuitive, inspired truth. Danton's "Open Field" self-communion (Scene 9) can be read back further than Faust's "Forest and Cavern" soliloquy; in fact, straight back to Hamlet's "To be, or not to be": as can Danton's monologue in Scene 19 (with touches of *Richard II*, III, 2). Several of the structural devices of *Hamlet* are evident. Ophelia's mad scene is recapitulated in Lucille's (Scene 19). The comic tumbril-driver recalls the first gravedigger (or the porter in *Macbeth*). The sudden humanizing of Robespierre (Scene 5) suggests Claudius' prayer scene. Indeed, the handling of Danton's hesitation might be cut from the whole fabric of *Hamlet*. However, the French Revolution cast itself in a Roman mold, and it is perhaps to Shakespeare's Roman plays, *Julius Caesar, Coriolanus,* and *Antony and Cleopatra* that one should turn, noting, as points of departure, the coarse, obscene, easily swayed mobs of the first two, the incessantly shuttled panorama of the last, and the reckless blind nobility of the hero in each.

What is missing is what we might expect a man infatuated with Shakespeare and writing about great events to produce: the passionate struggle, rich panoply, untrammeled idealism, and black and white ideology of the history plays. But it is as if Buechner conceived his central characters in Shakespeare's middle tragic vein—men who are probing, introspective, sickened by society—but set them down amid the shifting but inexorable external forces of the later plays. "Hamlet Goes to Rome" might make a good joking subtitle.

Nevertheless, for all its obvious and implicit borrowings, *Danton's Death* is loaded with characteristics that define its style as

Buechner's own: the deliberately abrupt transitions, the whiplash changes of mood, the frenetic flashing of locale changes, the erratic contrast in character portrayal in which one character seems fully fleshed in an instant and others reappear throughout without seeming to do more than represent a particular point of view. What should also be noted is the deliberate fashion in which Buechner seems to reconcile all the varied elements of the play. The plot is carefully manipulated to present, *first*, a series of actions which reflect history; *second*, the repercussions those historical actions create among a range of society; and *third*, the role, as actors and reactors, of the two dominant figures, Robespierre and Danton, and their respective seconds, St. Just and Camille Desmoulins. All three streams interweave, and if one is familiar with the principal figures of the Revolution (as Buechner's contemporaries were) the careful insertion of various individuals at crucial moments demonstrates Buechner's mastery at exposing and polishing the different facets of the Revolution (the Jacobins, for example, form a kind of daisy chain of calculated plotting throughout).

Buttressing this intricate structure is a solid conventional plot development. The play can be easily divided into four parts: I. Exposition of Forces; II. The Forces in Conflict; III. Resolution of Action; IV. Climax and Dénouement.

The rhythms of the play are set up by the interaction of the three plot streams of action, and are controlled by the four kinds of language Buechner uses: the great rhetorical speeches, both public and private; the civilized banter through which the deeply sincere sentiments of Danton's world are conveyed; the flat bureaucratic jargon of Robespierre's government men; and finally the robust but common talk of the proletariat, which actually represented a widespread attempt to catch a classical air and resulted in the so-called "Roman Republican speech," best demonstrated in the parody in Scene 1.

The play's thematic development emerges from its narrative concerns. Just as the course of the Revolution wanders in order to focus in the end on its major figures, making Danton stand for the Revolution, so the surface political material turns and twists until it finally produces a philosophical theory of life, a play which is really about death.

### III

Buechner's particular image of life as a political battlefield where the richer impulses towards experience are methodically annihilated by a frigid and merciless dogmatism is not uncommon in our own age. It is to be found both in those writers who study the idealistic man on the totalitarian rack of Communism, and those writers who see the common man throttled by the capitalistic system. Both tend to display a fundamental belief in social change through political action. However, the work of those writers who do not identify themselves with the possibility of political redemption, who postulate this eternal fruitless struggle against the dehumanizing processes of society as *the* condition of man might best be described, in Karl Vietor's phrase, as "heroic pessimism."

"Heroic pessimism" by no means defines the literature of the 1830's, for the transcendental movement in philosophy, the new discoveries in science, the rise of a new secularism in the Christian churches, and the materialistic gains of capitalism, were slowly taking hold to produce a new optimism that mastered all but the major literary figures of the century. Buechner's view of life, nevertheless, came straight from the age as he saw and experienced it.

Buechner grew up in the Early Victorian period called *Biedermeier* in Germany, a period characterized by the peace Metternich imposed after the successive hopes, bloodshed, and final resignation which the Napoleonic wars inspired. Throughout Europe, the republican optimism of the Revolution gave way to a dull, withdrawn, insular bourgeois philistinism. The liberal underground movements of the 1830's, spurred by the French overthrow of Charles X, petered out under stern police action or immovable middle-class inertia.

Buechner had joined such an underground movement in the Duchy of Hesse, a mildly socialist-nationalist conspiracy which collapsed through its own ineptitude and efficient police espionage. Buechner's contribution comprised some violent revolutionary pamphletry, *The Hessian Rural Messenger*. He had rejected the idealistic appeal to the educated classes that most liberal movements thrive on. "Our time is strictly materialistic," he claimed, and no "well-to-do minority" would ever "give up its privileged position to the great masses. And what of those masses? For them there are only two levers: want and religious fanaticism." Accordingly, he framed his appeal to the peasants in surprisingly Marxist economic terms, and urged the peasants to seize the means of production for themselves. An abortive insurrection in Frankfort, the peasants' habit of turning over the perilously distributed pamphlets to the police, and the remarkable effectiveness of a stool pigeon in his own League for the Rights of Man, which earmarked Buechner for prison, led to his exile and disillusionment. His subsequent letters regard the revolutionary movements as "ridiculous," "absurd," or "a farce," but his vision of lower-class behavior as predicated on economic want and irrational fanaticism shape the horrifying and historically accurate portrait of the mob in *Danton's Death*.

The temptation to read something autobiographical into Buechner's portrait of Danton is obvious, just as one can see Hamlet in both of them. The man of vision, educated to find new values in life, runs afoul of an unyielding world which is treacherous, wily, unethical, and blindly committed to ways of life he cannot penetrate. He finds himself isolated, incapable of action, disgusted and amused by the absurdity of it all, and is finally destroyed; irrevocably cast as the lifegiving spirit of the law who fails to put down the Pharisees and dies in the struggle that truth may live.

It was natural for Buechner to turn to the French Revolution to solve the puzzle of his own age. By 1825 it had become safe to study the Revolution dispassionately. The historians of the day like those of the 1920's, attempted to sort out the larger patterns of action in history and to discern in them the measurable, and therefore predictable, forces that govern historical events, in order to control contemporary ones. The nineteenth-century historians saw life as moving through the agency of powerful individuals and so produced great biographical studies, documented in impressive scholarly detail.

Buechner's instinct was somewhat different. He saw history as the product of deterministic but capricious and essentially uncontrollable forces. Throughout his plays man is pictured as a living puppet, helplessly aware of the strings that move him, finding in the actions imposed on him a vision of distant unknown forces, at best experiencing the richness of existence while acknowledging his status as a clown in the circus of the gods. In *Danton's Death* he has used this viewpoint to search out the true nature of the great figures involved and to identify the forces that motivated them.

In doing so, he made use of three writers, Mignet, Thiers, and Strahlheim. A surprising amount of *Danton's Death* is straight history. Some of the public speeches are based on actual reports. But it is astounding to see how Buechner, by slight twists, by inspired additions, and by ingenious extensions of facts, events, and personalities produced his own French Revolution, one that in many ways rings more true than that of the historians.

Buechner's two leading characters are not quite as accurate as historical evidence suggests. Danton's contemporaries agreed that Danton was "hardy in soul . . . inexhaustibly resourceful," "audacious," and, at the same time, "lazy and voluptuous," which sustains the paradox Buechner uses to represent Danton. But others noted a "cruel and repulsive face" which "perfectly characterized the frenzy of brutal passions." And it seems beyond dispute that Danton lived comfortably on graft, condoned the "September Massacres" on which Robespierre capitalized, and encouraged the early acts of terrorism. The latter facts Buechner only implies, as if Danton's previous deeds were unimportant, as if Danton can only be defined as he felt and behaved at a certain point in life, once he had discovered the truth about existence and set about to live out that truth meaningfully.

Nor was Robespierre exactly the character Buechner painted, but rather more of an opportunist, more vacillating; his great speech in Scene 12, borrowed in part from real life by Buechner, was one of his rare decisive utterances. Foolishly rather than intellectually dogmatic, probably more manipulated than manipulating, he was nevertheless the figurehead of his time and if he comes across full blown as an incredibly ominous figure, the invention is not altogether Buechner's, for Robespierre was greater than life, as an image in men's eyes, and therefore as a dramatic character. Buechner only provided him with the traits, appetites, and will that make a man of the figure.

## IV

To convert history into drama, Buechner found it essential that Robespierre, the villain of the piece, be given strength and justice. His demagogic power, indeed the power of all demagogues, is demonstrated in one sharp speech (Scene 1) and his first sentence before the Jacobin Club (Scene 3): "We have waited to speak only to hear the cry of indignation sound all around us," has the stamp of the effective despot. In Scene 5, he is humanized for a few stirring moments, and given an inner life that is both so unreal and integral that it can only be understood in terms of modern psychology. It seems almost clinical in its revelation of the kind of damaged psychopath who projects his vengeful aggressive impulses on to others, and sees himself as a god-appointed instrument of justice who can do no wrong. But however perfect the case history, the imagery of Robespierre conjures the truths of poetry. His picture of "Night snores over the earth, wallowing in its barren dreams," his notion of life as an ugly dream, an extension of the sins of the mind, and his final recognition that he is a kind of antichrist, superior to the Savior: "I have the torment of the executioner. Who has denied himself more? He or I? . . . The son of man is crucified in us all . . . the world is barren . . . empty—I am alone," convey the nature of Robespierre in a way neither psychology nor history can manage.

Robespierre is caught in the one impossible task of political action, that of continuing a revolution after it has succeeded. Revolutions begin with ideals, then seek to enforce those ideals on society. But revolutionists are by nature rebels, incapable of yielding to the rigid demands of the state, even when it is the result of their own action, and the man who tries to make the revolution work winds up by killing off his fellow revolutionaries. He must suddenly chastise men for their weakness, and ignore their value, their past, their humanity. He becomes the victim of his own abstractions, and sacrifices everything to the righteousness of his own behavior. "Robespierre is the dogma of the Revolution" says Danton. "Virtue must rule through terror," says Robespierre. "Conscience is a mirror for a monkey to make soulful faces at," replies Danton, and marks himself for destruction. For Robespierre believes that "whoever trembles at this moment is guilty." Those who fail to affirm the actions of the government are conspirators, enemies of the state. An old story, but Robespierre draws it to its logical conclusion. He was known as the Incorruptible, but the Incorruptible, to be true to himself, was obliged to destroy every sign of doubt in others until there was nothing left that might corrupt him.

In the face of political totalitarianism, Danton chooses life, or rather living. The senses are real; our feelings are all we have, becomes his credo. "We are all only epicures, coarse or fine," he proclaims, and adds "Christ was the finest" (Scene 5). In the face of coercion, in the absence of faith, in the knowledge that we can't control our destiny, he advocates saying what one thinks, feeling what one feels, experiencing whatever existence we possess, even if we are somebody else's creation. "We spend our lives on the stage. Only the death scene at the end is real" (Scene 6). And against the implication of eternal values in his heroically ironic final words, uttered when the executioner tries to prevent him from embracing his friend: "Would you be more terrible than death? You can't keep our heads from kissing at the bottom of the basket," (Scene 21) one must place the resigned recognition of "there is no hope in death, it is only a simpler, less organized form of corruption than life."

Throughout the last half of the play the alternating themes of the cruelty of historic action and the humanity of its victims take on increasing intensity and provide rich variation on Camille Desmoulins' earlier perception that "I am sent to the scaffold because my eyes could still get wet at the fate of our miserable people" (Scene 13).

But *Danton's Death* is an unsentimental play. Buechner permits no one to come off well. Danton's friends have their frailties. There are fools on his side, too. And at their moments of greatest sincerity, Danton and his friends recognize their vanity. There is no way to see this play simply. We can view it historically as a climactic point in western civilization when the residual situation of a period of human idealism evoked a kind of rigorous, joking skepticism. We can see it as an existential effort to find traces of meaningfulness in a world where life is only a slower form of death. We can read it as a confused testament of romanticism, in which the author cannot choose between proclaiming the ultimate truth of the senses or seeking after supernatural truth. Or we can dismiss it as a sensitive but chaotic borrowing and amalgamation of great ideas, great perceptions, and great plays by an ebullient young man.

To understand *Danton's Death* requires making order where order does not really exist but begs to be discovered. Its creator is bitter, mocking, spirited, unpredictable, and teasingly profound. The same is true of many great minds. Buechner died young, and whether the promise he showed would have been realized is only a matter for speculation. But critics have not begun to exhaust the meaning of *Danton's Death*. And since it also continues to attract them, it is perhaps on its way to becoming acknowledged as a great play, the kind of great play which can never be resolved or reduced because it is also a great mystery.

THEODORE HOFFMAN

# Danton's Death

DANTON
CAMILLE DESMOULINS
HÉRAULT-SÉCHELLES } Deputies of the National Convention
LACROIX
PHILIPPEAU
LEGENDRE

ROBESPIERRE
ST. JUST
BARÈRE } Members of the Committee of Public Safety
COLLOT D'HERBOIS
BILLAUD-VARENNES

FOUQUIER-TINVILLE, the public prosecutor
TOM PAINE, an English philosopher
CHAUMETTE, a defrocked monk
SIMON, a theatrical prompter
GENERAL DILLON
LAFLOTTE, a citizen
A DEPUTY FROM LYONS
THE PRESIDENT OF THE NATIONAL CONVENTION
A BEGGAR
A WAITER
A JUDGE OF THE REVOLUTIONARY TRIBUNAL

JULIE, Danton's wife
LUCILLE, Camille's wife

MARION
ROSALIE } prostitutes
AURORE

SIMON'S WIFE
EUGÉNIE
A VIRTUOUS LADY
A MARCHIONESS

GAOLERS, EXECUTIONERS, SOLDIERS, SERVANTS, and other CITIZENS of the Republic of France.

# PART ONE

## Scene One

[*A Street. A queue of citizens, women and some men, waiting for bread. One of the women has a piece of dirty rich material which she uses for a shawl.* SIMON, *drunk, is looking for his* WIFE. *He sees her, starts to beat her, and tears the cloth off her back.*]

SIMON   Ha! Long live the Republic!—Ah! Filthy traitress!—Aristocrat lover! . . . worm-eaten apple of sin!

WIFE   Oh! Oh— Help! Help!

[CITIZENS *rush to separate them.*]

CITIZENS   Stop him! Part them!—Hold him! Hold him down!

SIMON   Let me go! I'll break her bones!—I'll tear the filthy silk from her back! I'll fling her carcass naked in the gutter!—Oh! . . . whore!—every wrinkle of your body is a nest of lewdness!

[SIMON *is pinned down.*]

A CITIZEN   What's the matter?

SIMON   Where is my little girl?—Girl? No, never again! . . . my daughter!—Oh, no! . . . there is only one name for her now—it chokes me! I have no breath to speak it!

A CITIZEN   If he had, his daughter's name would smell of cognac.

[SIMON *weeps.*]

WIFE   Let him go now. The fit's over. H   can't hold much, you know. He'll pass out in a minute.

SIMON   Vampire's tooth! You drink my blood.

WIFE   He's a mean man. But he's not crazy really. He gets into a sweat with his work—he prompts the actors at the theater. And he drinks in all their nonsense with the cognac.

SIMON   Ah! Vestal!

WIFE   Don't you call me your filthy names!—I'm afraid he's always been a dirty-minded man.

SIMON [*tragically, passionately*]
   "Ah, Virginius, cover your old grey head!
   The Raven Shame doth light upon your brow
   To peck out your old eyes" . . .
Ah, my little Lucretia!—Give me a dagger, Romans!

3

[*He collapses.*]

WIFE There, he's gone now.

BILLAUD [*coming in*] What happened?

WIFE Well, you see—I was waiting for our bread, and my daughter—he calls her Lucretia, but she was christened Jeanne-Marie—she went off walking with a young gentleman—she's a good girl, she thinks only of her parents.

SIMON Ah!—she confesses!

WIFE You Judas! Would you have a pair of pants to put on if the gentlemen didn't take theirs off with her? You sponge—you'd thirst to death if she ran as dry as you.—We work with what part of us works best—why not with that one? Her mother worked when she came into the world, and painful work it was. Can't she do a bit for her mother, eh? And do you think she's feeling any pain? You—

SIMON Ah, my Lucretia! A dagger, Romans, a dagger!

[*He passes out completely.*]

BILLAUD Yes, a dagger!—but not for the poor whore! What has she done? Nothing! Her hunger is a whore and a beggar. A dagger for the gentlemen, who buy the flesh of our wives and daughters!—You have hunger pains, they have indigestion! You have holes in your clothes, they have warm coats! You have calluses on your hands, they have silk gloves! You work, and they are idle, and what you earn they steal. And when you want a few pennies of your stolen earnings back, you have to beg from them and whore with them to get it. They are thieves! Strike them down!

CITIZENS There's no blood in their veins—except what they've sucked from us. When they were poor like us, they said, Strike down the aristocrats, the aristocrats are wolves! they said. In September we killed the aristocrats—we hung an aristocrat from every lamppost in Paris! The Girondins are starving you, they said. We dragged the Girondins in cartloads to the guillotine.

BILLAUD But who looted the corpses? They did, and now they are aristocrats. And you stand here as naked as before and freeze to death. Another September! Strike the new aristocrats!

CITIZENS September! Strike the new aristocrats! September!

A CITIZEN We must tear the skin off their backs to make ourselves trousers, we must boil the fat of their buttocks to make ourselves soup! Kill them!

A Citizen   Death to the man with no hole in his coat!

A Citizen   Kill the gentlemen with satin trousers!

A Citizen   Kill the men who can read and write!

[A Young Gentleman *enters.*]

Wife   He has a handkerchief! An aristocrat!

Billaud   Hang him! Hang him from the lamp-post!

Wife [*snatching the handkerchief*]   Can't you blow your nose with your fingers?—Hang him from the lamppost!

[*A lamp is let down.*]

Young Gentleman   Oh!—Gentlemen!

Billaud   There are no gentlemen here! To the lamppost!

[*They sing while the noose is being tied. The* Young Gentleman *is lifted up.*]

Young Gentleman   Mercy!

A Citizen   It's only a game—your feet mustn't touch the ground. It will be over in a minute. We are more merciful than you. We hang at the end of the string for sixty years, and kick. But now we're cutting ourselves down! Up—up to the lamp!

Citizens   Hang him from the lamp!

Young Gentleman [*terrified*]   It won't shine any brighter because of me!

[*There is a roar of laughter and cheers from the crowd, and some confusion, in which the* Young Gentleman *is dropped on the ground. He tears away. Some* Citizens *go after him.*]

A Few Citizens   Let him go!

[Robespierre *enters.*]

Robespierre   What is it, citizens?

A Citizen   Our wives and children cry out for bread!

Citizens   Bread!

Billaud   We'll feed them with the flesh of the new aristocrats!

A Woman   Does the guillotine buy us bread?

Citizens   Strike down our enemies! The guillotine is too slow! Kill the men with no holes in their coats! Kill them! Kill them!

Robespierre   In the name of the law!

A CITIZEN   What is the law?

ROBESPIERRE   The will of the people.

A CITIZEN   We are the people. And we want no law. That's the will of the people! Kill them!

SOME CITIZENS   Hear the Incorruptible! Hear Robespierre! Hear the Incorruptible!

A WOMAN   Hear the Messiah, who is sent to be our voice and our judge. He will strike our enemies with the sharpness of his sword. His eyes are the eyes of truth, his hands are the hands of justice.

ROBESPIERRE   Poor, virtuous people! You do your duty. You sacrifice your enemies. People, you are great! You reveal yourselves in lightning flash and thunderbolt. But, people, your vengeance must not fall on your own heads. In your most righteous rage you wound yourselves. Your enemies know that you can only fall by your own strength. But your legislators are on watch, they will guide your hands, their eyes shall never be deceived, your arms shall never slacken. We shall not rest!—Come with me to your Jacobin brothers. They shall welcome you with open arms. We shall hold a bloody judgment on our enemies!

CITIZENS   Long live Robespierre!—To the Jacobin Club! Long live Robespierre!

[*The* CITIZENS *follow* ROBESPIERRE. SIMON *is lying on the ground, his* WIFE *sitting beside him.*]

SIMON [*moans*]   Oh—all alone!

WIFE [*helping him up*]   There, then . . .

SIMON   Oh, my Baucis, you pour coals of fire on my head.

WIFE [*dropping him*]   Help yourself, then!

SIMON   Oh!—Don't leave me!—Can you forgive me, Portia?— Did I beat you? . . . Not I. My madness beat you . . . "His madness is poor Hamlet's enemy."—Where is my little girl?

WIFE   This way—round the corner.

SIMON [*unwilling to go*]   Oh, my Lucretia!

WIFE   Well?

SIMON   Come, my virtuous wife.

[*They go off.*]

## Scene Two

[*A room in* DANTON'S *house.* HÉRAULT-SÉCHELLES *is playing cards at a table with a* MARCHIONESS *and a* COUNTESS. DANTON *is seated on a foot-stool at the feet of his wife,* JULIE.]

MARCHIONESS [*to the* COUNTESS, *playing a card*]   We have lost our king!

COUNTESS [*playing a card*]   The queen falls with him!

HÉRAULT [*taking the trick, playing a card*]   The knave is high!

[*The* MARCHIONESS *gathers the cards and shuffles.*]

DANTON   See—the pretty lady, how cleverly she plays her cards. They say she never deals a heart except to her husband, though she takes all kinds of tricks in diamonds from other men.— Wives! You can even make us love such a lie.

JULIE   Do you believe in *me*?

DANTON   How do I know? We know very little of each other. We are thick-skinned creatures—we stretch out our hands, but what is the use of rubbing our hides together?—we are very lonely.

JULIE   You know me, Danton.

DANTON   Yes, they call it knowing. You have dark eyes and curly hair and a delicate skin and you always say to me: dear George! . . . but there [*he touches her forehead and eyelids*] . . . there . . . what lies in there?—Ah . . . we have coarse senses. Know each other? We would have to break our skulls open and tear the thoughts from our brain cells.

[HÉRAULT *is playing with the* MARCHIONESS'S *hand.*]

MARCHIONESS   What are you doing with your fingers?

HÉRAULT   Nothing.

MARCHIONESS   Your thumb has very crude manners.

HÉRAULT [*holding up thumb*]   Why?—because he always stands up in the company of ladies?

DANTON   No, Julie, I love you like the grave.

JULIE [*turning away*]   Oh!

DANTON   No, listen. People say—we shall find peace in the grave . . . when I lie in your lap, I am under the earth already. You sweet grave, your lips are funeral bells, your voice is my death knell, your breast is the mound of my grave, your heart my coffin.

*[The ladies and* HÉRAULT *have finished another hand.]*

MARCHIONESS *[to* HÉRAULT] Lost!

HÉRAULT *[putting down money]* It was an amorous adventure. Like all the others, it costs money.

MARCHIONESS Then you have declared your love, like a deaf-mute, with your fingers.

HÉRAULT And I hope I was not misunderstood.

[PHILIPPEAU, CAMILLE DESMOULINS, *and* LACROIX *come in.*]

HÉRAULT Philippeau—with a tragic face! Did it rain during the guillotining? Or did you get such a bad seat you couldn't see anything?

CAMILLE He lost his red cap and had to be sent home before the end.

PHILIPPEAU Forty heads fell today. Tomorrow there will be more. St. Just has set a limit of fifty a day. The executioners are overworked, and the Committee has to slaughter according to schedule.

CAMILLE They make cavemen of us. St. Just would have us crawl on all fours to our lessons in virtue, and worship Robespierre, the Schoolmistress, for our God.

LACROIX Someone must speak out. The Committee of Public Safety is becoming all-powerful. The Convention is paralyzed. Danton is never there.

HÉRAULT He is ashamed to appear among the legislators he has castrated. He created the Committee because making laws took up too much of his time.

LACROIX And now the Committee is Robespierre's pulpit. Danton sits meekly in the congregation with the rest of Paris.—"Virtue must rule through terror."—After the sermon the list of the accused.

PHILIPPEAU The Revolution is still a new-born monster child—bloody and foul—we are cradled in coffins, and left to play with a string of human heads.

LACROIX The committee must be overruled. The tyranny of blood must end! The people want bread, they will listen to us. In September, when Danton cried, "The Republic is in danger," they tore down the walls of their houses for gunpowder, they made cannons out of melted coffins and church bells. When Camille appointed himself Attorney General of the Lamppost, they hanged a thousand aristocrats in the name of the Revolution.

PHILIPPEAU  The Revolution must give way to the Republic. Freedom must live in peace.

HÉRAULT  Every man has a right to live his life according to his nature. Virtue! A man ought to be virtuous or vile as he chooses, what does it matter to the Republic? We are all fools—no fool has the right to say, do as I do. The principle of freedom is: take your pleasure at your own risk, and don't get in anyone else's way while you're doing it.

CAMILLE  The Republic must be worn on the body of the people like a tight-fitting transparent dress. Every movement of her flesh, every breath of longing, must be seen. Let her figure be beautiful or ugly—she has the right to show herself for what she is—who are we to cut her wardrobe to our fancy? Anyone who can look at the naked shoulders of our beloved sinner, France, and want to throw a nun's veil over her, gets his fingers rapped. The new society must have naked gods—no fig leaves—Olympic games, orgies, hymns sung by melodious lips in praise of loose and luscious love. Anyone who wants to be a Roman can sit in the corner and cook turnips. But no more gladiators, no more throwing to the lions. And as the symbol of our liberties—over the door of the Republic the beautiful buttocks of Venus shall rest in perfect freedom.—Danton, you shall proclaim the new Republic in the Convention!

DANTON  I shall, thou shalt, he shall . . . if we are spared, as the old ladies say. In an hour sixty minutes will have flown away. Right, my boy?

CAMILLE  Right, that goes without saying.

DANTON  Everything goes without saying.—And who shall bring all these beautiful things to pass?

PHILIPPEAU  We—and the honest people.

DANTON  That "and" is a long word, it keeps a fair distance between us. The honest people might run out of breath before they catch up with us.—And if they did, what could we do, with them on our hands? Honest people! You can lend money to them, be godfather to their children, and you can marry your daughter to them—But that's all!

CAMILLE  If you believe that, why did you fight for the people in the first place?

DANTON  [shrugs]  They drove me mad . . . I was itching to kick somebody. It's my nature.

[He gets up.]

JULIE  You're going?

DANTON  They rub me the wrong way with their politics.—I'll make you a prophecy: The statue of Freedom is not yet moulded, but the furnace is lit. All of us might still get our fingers burnt. —The lesson of the Revolution is: we are suspect, you are suspect, they are suspect.

[*He goes out.*]

CAMILLE  Let him go!—Do you think he'll be able to keep his fingers to himself, if the Republic is in danger?

HÉRAULT  No. He'll need a pastime. But something livelier than playing cards.

## Scene Three

[*The Jacobin Club.* ROBESPIERRE *and* ST. JUST *with some* CITIZENS, LACROIX *and* HÉRAULT *together,* LEGENDRE *and some* DEPUTIES, *including a* DEPUTY *from the city of Lyons.*]

BILLAUD  Have you read the *Cordelier?*—Camille has written an open letter to Robespierre.

COLLOT  What does he say?

CITIZEN  He is mad, Camille.

COLLOT  "Oh, my friend Robespierre—I address myself to you— my old school-friend, my dear comrade—do you remember our lessons in history and philosophy? How we were taught that love is stronger and more lasting than fear, that mercy is the cherished attribute of power, that the most virtuous men can never climb to Heaven on steps that drip with blood? You who sit on the Committee of Public Safety, it is to preserve our new liberties from despotism that I take up my pen as a weapon against you. Our poor Republic of prisons! Sick of the guillotine! Surely now it must be worthy of a Committee of Mercy—Or is mercy now a crime in this Republic—Only a despotism joins the hands of patriots and traitors under the guillotine! Mercy for the sons of the Revolution! Mercy for the liberties of France!"

DEPUTY FROM LYONS  Your mercy murders the Revolution— Citizens of Paris! Your brothers of Lyons can take no cowardly view of justice. Lyons, which was the whore of kings and aristocrats, the plaything of the Girondins, shall rise bleeding but pure. The traitors have fallen. They shall never come again. Pitt's cargo of royalists in the Mediterranean shall never spoil our city. The Rhone shall flow with blood, the British fleet shall founder on shoals of corpses! The justice of Lyons shall be bloody and

unashamed!—mercy? To us the breath of a single aristocrat is
the death rattle of freedom. Mercy is counterrevolution. Only
cowards would die for the Republic, the Jacobin virtue is to kill
for her.—In Lyons a Jacobin asks himself, have you done enough
to be hanged if counterrevolution comes? If it comes, all your
brothers of Lyons stand condemned of having served their country! Our city shall be buried in the bones of traitors sooner than
show herself a stain on the soil of France!

[*Acclamation.*]

LEGENDRE   We need not look to Lyons for instruction in recog-
nising traitors. They are plain enough! They wear silk clothes,
they drive in carriages to adorn the boxes of theatres, they carry
their heads so proudly that they dare to shrug their shoulders.
They are witty, and say, the guillotine has passed us by. For now
the rabble execute each other. Only heroes of the Revolution
tread the scaffold now—

JACOBIN [*loudly*]   Who has lost his head that was not a traitor?
The Revolution has no heroes!

LEGENDRE   I call upon the present members of the Committee of
Public Safety—has Hébert never served his country? Ronsin?
Mormore?

ST. JUST   And I call upon you, Legendre, to confess—whose voice
gives you such large breath for speaking treason! It is time to
tear off the masks! The puppet has betrayed his master. The
committee sees through you, Legendre.

JACOBINS   For whom does Legendre speak? Who are the traitors?

[ROBESPIERRE *makes a motion to speak.*]

ST. JUST   Hear the Incorruptible! Hear Robespierre!

ROBESPIERRE   We have waited to speak only to hear the cry of
indignation sound all around us. Our eyes were open, we saw the
enemy take arms and rise up, but we have not given the alarm.
We let the people watch over itself, it has not slept, it has taken
arms and made clamor. We have made the enemy abandon his
ambush, we have made him approach. Now he stands boldly
uncovered in the bright light of day. As soon as you have looked
upon him, he is dead. This subtlest enemy of the Republic has
only one weapon—his weakness; his battle cry, which we now
have heard, is a whimper for mercy. But he will snatch the
weapons from the people's hands, he will suck our strength, to
yield us up naked and unnerved into the hands of royal tyrants.
The weapon of the Republic is terror, the strength of the Republic is virtue!—virtue, because without it terror is a disease—

terror, because without it virtue is paralysed. Terror is the child of virtue—it is nothing else but justice, sudden, strong, and most implacable.

They will tell you that terror is the weapon of a despotic regime. True! The Revolution is the despotism of freedom against tyranny.

Mercy for the royalists! they cry.

Mercy for monsters?—no! Mercy for the downtrodden, mercy for the innocent, mercy for the weak, mercy for humanity! Only the peaceful citizen deserves the protection of society. In a Republic the citizens are republicans; royalists and foreigners are enemies. To punish the oppressors of humanity is mercy; to pardon them is criminal. The citizen who gives way to false sentimentality is sighing in the direction of England and Austria.

But these enemies are not content to disarm our virtuous people. They seek to sap our strength at its most sacred source—to poison us with vice. This is their most subtle, dangerous, and horrifying attack upon our freedom. Only the most hellish monsters— . . . but no! I will not say it was deliberate. This shameful moral poison may be involuntary, but the effect is the same, the danger is as great! Vice is the mark of Cain that brands the aristocracy. Those who practise vice are the political enemies of freedom; and the greater the services they appear to have rendered, the more suspect are their crimes. The most dangerous citizen is the man who would sooner wear out a dozen red caps than restrain himself to virtuous deeds.

You will understand me easily, if you think of citizens who once lived in garrets that now parade in carriages with all the vicious luxury of erstwhile courtiers, keep servants, give luxurious banquets, wear rich clothes, and with former marchionesses practise vice. Legislators of the people! Now counts and princes of the Revolution! They demoralize the sublime drama of the Revolution to a parody in debauch.

No mercy for citizens who speculate in the Revolution! No acquittal for citizens who hoped to plunder the people and go unpunished!

Our enemies stand in the erupting stream of the terror. They will not cool its justice by saying, "We are not virtuous enough to be so terrible! Have mercy on our weakness. We dare not confess that we are vicious, we would rather say that you are cruel!"

Rest easy, virtuous people! Take heart, you patriots! Say to your brothers of Lyons: the sword of justice will never rust in the hand that with your strength shall swing it! We will make the Republic a great example!

JACOBINS  Long live the Republic! Long live Robespierre!

[ROBESPIERRE *is followed out by all the* JACOBINS. HÉRAULT *also leaves* LACROIX *and follows* ROBESPIERRE. *Only* LEGENDRE *and* LACROIX *remain.*]

LACROIX     What have you done, Legendre?—You have shrugged your shoulders. Do you know whose heads will topple?

LEGENDRE     Some fashionable citizens and their women. That's all.

LACROIX     I thought St. Just made it clear enough. You were a shadow, he said. And you have betrayed the man to whom you owed your existence. You have committed suicide!

LEGENDRE     What do you mean?

LACROIX     Whom do you think Robespierre meant by princes of the Revolution?—The Committee is in trouble. They must stage a glamorous show on the guillotine. They have sent a few dusty atheists, the madmen of the Revolution, on to the platform. But the people are not impressed. They run barefoot through the streets, screaming for skins of quality for shoe leather. The popularity of the guillotine must not drop, or the Committee itself will go to a very cold exit on the boards.

LEGENDRE     What have I done?

LACROIX     You have given them a "counter-revolution"; you have shown them where to point the finger.

LEGENDRE     Where is Danton?

LACROIX     Who knows?—Probably he's collecting pieces of the Medici Venus from all the whores in the Palais-Royal. He's making a mosaic. It's very difficult, he says, Nature has so smashed the ideal of beauty and scattered the pieces in so many bodies. God knows what piece he's after now.—Let's go to the Palais-Royal.

## Scene Four

[*Marion's room in the Palais-Royal.* MARION *and* DANTON *are on a bed.* MARION *moves to get away.*]

MARION     No—let me go! . . . I want to talk to you.

DANTON     Your lips have a better use than that.

MARION     No, let me be—My mother was a good woman. She used to say to me, modesty is the most beautiful virtue. When people came to our house—sometimes when they were talking, my mother made me leave the room. If I asked her what they'd meant, she told me I ought to be ashamed of myself. Whenever she gave me a book to read, I always had to skip some pages.

But I loved to read the Bible, and everything in that was holy
. . . but some things I didn't understand. I couldn't ask anybody,
I thought about them by myself. Then, one year . . . spring came,
and there was something happening all round me, in which I had
no part . . . but I had to breathe in the strange atmosphere of it
that nearly smothered me. I would look at my body . . . I felt
torn in two and melted together again.—A boy used to come to
the house. He was pretty, and said foolish things. I never knew
what they meant, but they made me laugh. My mother asked
him often—that was all right with us. Finally we couldn't see—
if we could sit with each other on two chairs, why couldn't we lie
together between two sheets? . . . And he made me happier than
with his talking, and I couldn't see why they should let us do
the foolish things and not the thing that made us happy. We did
it secretly. We went on doing it . . . but then—I was like a sea,
that swallows everything and drags it deeper and deeper. There
was only one thing that I could feel—all men melted into one
body. It was my nature. How can you escape yourself? . . . he
sensed it finally. One morning he came, and he kissed me as if he
wanted to strangle me, he squeezed my neck, it was horrible to
be so frightened. Then he let me go, and laughed, and said he'd
almost done something stupid—I should keep my dress on, and
look after it, it would wear out soon enough, and he didn't want
to spoil the joke for me beforehand but it was the only thing I
had left in the world . . . then he went away, and I never knew
what he'd meant . . . That evening I was sitting at my window—
I am very sentimental I only understand things by how I feel . . .
I was dreaming in the red cloudy sunset. And a crowd came up
the street, children running ahead, and women looking out of
their windows. I looked down—they carried him by in a basket,
the moon shone on his white forehead, his hair was wet, he had
drowned himself. I had to cry.—It was the only shock I have
ever felt . . . other people have Sundays and working days, six
days for living and one for praying, they feel something on their
birthdays and when the New Year comes. I don't understand
that. I feel no change, no holidays, I am one thing always, an
endless longing and grasping, a fire, a stream, a hunger. My
mother died of horror . . . people pointed their fingers at me . . .
that's stupid . . . we all have pleasure in something—in bodies,
in pictures of Christ, in flowers, in playing games . . . the longing is the same . . . the people that get the most pleasure have
to pray the most . . .

DANTON  Why can't I hold all the beauty of you inside me?

MARION  Danton, your lips have eyes.

DANTON   I want to be a piece of the air, to bathe all about you, to break myself on every part of your body.

[LACROIX *comes in, followed by* AURORE *and* ROSALIE.]

LACROIX [*laughing*]   It's funny . . . it's very funny . . .

DANTON [*unwillingly*]   What?

LACROIX   In the street . . .

DANTON   Yes?

LACROIX   . . . two dogs, a Great Dane and a terrier, torturing each other.

DANTON   Well . . .

LACROIX   I just remembered it, and I had to laugh, it was so elevating. Little girls looking out of the windows—parents should be more careful, they let them sit in the sun. The flies will do it on their hands, that will make them think about it.—Legendre and I have been looking through the cells. The nuns here are so pious in their devotion to the revelation through the flesh—they all hung on our coats and begged for the blessing. Legendre is running through the service with one of them. Well, he's been fasting for a month.—Here are a couple of fanatical priestesses that desire my salvation.

MARION   Good day, Miss Aurore. Good day, Miss Rosalie.

ROSALIE   It's a long time since we've had the pleasure.

MARION   I'm very sorry.

AURORE   Oh, God, we're busy night and day.

DANTON [*to* ROSALIE]   Eh, my child—your hips are growing very worth-while.

ROSALIE   Oh, yes—we get a little more perfect every day.

DANTON   And Aurore has become very quaint and modest. A charming new development—Her face is like a fig leaf that she holds up in front of herself. Like a cool patch of shade on a busy street.

AURORE [*irritated*]   I would be the busiest street in Paris, if you wanted to . . .

DANTON [*interrupting*]   I know—don't be angry, little darling.— Little Rosalie is a restored torso—only the hips and ankles are really antique.

LACROIX   Two sisters of mercy, each serving in her own private hospital.

ROSALIE [*to* AURORE] They ought to be ashamed. They make me blush.

AURORE They have no manners.

[*They go out.*]

DANTON Good night, pretty children!—I'm sorry for them, they came for their supper.

LACROIX Listen, Danton, I've been to the Jacobin Club.

DANTON Have you nothing better to do?

LACROIX Camille's article on mercy was read out. That brought a tirade from a deputy from Lyons. Legendre cried out that the Revolution is murdering those who served it best.—He lost his head. He's come right out in the open against the terror.

DANTON And Robespierre?

LACROIX Pursed his lips and said "Virtue must rule through Terror." The phrase gives me a pain.

DANTON They are trimming planks for the platform of the guillotine.

LACROIX St. Just chanted something about tearing off the masks.

DANTON The faces will come off with them.

[HÉRAULT *comes in.*]

LACROIX What's happening?

HÉRAULT I went from the club to see Robespierre. I demanded an explanation. He tried to make a face like Brutus sacrificing his children. He spoke abstractly about duty, and said where freedom was concerned he would hear of no discrimination, he would sacrifice everything—himself, his brothers, and his friends.

DANTON Yes, but he'll change the order of the service and step down to help his friends up first.—We must be grateful to Legendre, he has made them speak up.

LACROIX The people are still miserably poor. If the committee can't give them bread, they'll have to stage a circus. They'll have to balance the scales. They need a heavy head.

DANTON I know.—The Revolution is like Saturn, it eats its own children.—But they wouldn't dare.

LACROIX Danton, you are a dead saint. The Revolution smashes idols. They've thrown Christ out of the churches, they've tossed the bones of the king into the gutter. Do you think they'll let you stand as a national monument?

DANTON   My name!—The people!

LACROIX   Your name! You are a moderate. So am I, so is Hérault, and Camille and Philippeau. To the people moderation is the same as weakness. The section leaders—every redcap in Paris—will feel betrayed if Robespierre can make them believe that Danton the hero of September is a moderate after all.

DANTON   You're right . . . and the people are like a child, they have to break everything, to see if there is anything inside.

LACROIX   And, Danton, we are vicious, as Robespierre says. We live only for pleasure. And the people are virtuous. They don't live only for pleasure.

HÉRAULT   They can't. They don't drink because they haven't any money. They don't go to brothels because they smell of cheese and herring and the girls won't have them.

DANTON   They hate us as a eunuch hates men.

LACROIX   They say we are idle, and rich, we live off the Republic like parasites. And between you and me, there's something in what they say.—Robespierre and the people will agree to remain virtuous, St. Just will intone the funeral oration, the Convention will put on a sacrificial toga, and . . . I see it all!

DANTON   You're dreaming. They have never had any courage without me, they have none to use against me. The Revolution is not finished, they might just find they need me.—They will keep me in a glass case.

LACROIX   We must act!

DANTON   We'll see.

[*He kisses* MARION.]

LACROIX   We'll see the blade falling!

MARION   Your lips are cold, you have smothered your kisses with words.

DANTON   [*to* MARION]   To have lost so much time! . . . it was worth the trouble. [*to* LACROIX] Tomorrow I'll go and see Robespierre. I'll make him angry, and we'll see what's in his mind.—Tomorrow, then! Good night, my friends, good night and thank you.

LACROIX   Begone, my friends, begone!—Good night, Danton. The thighs of a whore are your guillotine.

[LACROIX *goes out.* HÉRAULT *follows.*]

## Scene Five

[*A room in* ROBESPIERRE'S *house.* ROBESPIERRE, *with* DANTON,
HÉRAULT, *and* LACROIX.]

ROBESPIERRE  I tell you, the man who tries to embrace me when
I am drawing my sword is my enemy—his good intentions are
nothing to me; if he keeps me from defending myself, he kills
me as surely as if he attacked me.

DANTON  Where self-defence leaves off, murder begins. I see no
principle that forces us to go on killing each other.

ROBESPIERRE  The social revolution is not yet complete. If you
leave a Revolution half-finished, you dig your own grave. The
society of exploitation is not yet dead. Instead of the maze of
titillated classes, the people in its wholesome strength must stand
alone. Vice must be punished. Virtue must rule through terror.

DANTON  I don't understand the word *punish.*—Your virtue,
Robespierre! You have accepted no money, you have contracted
no debts, you have slept with no women, you always wear a
respectable coat, and you never get drunk. Robespierre, you are
appallingly virtuous. I would be ashamed to mince along between
Heaven and earth for thirty years, making the same moral face,
simply for the miserable satisfaction of finding everyone else
nastier than me. Is there nothing inside you, nothing at all, that
whispers to you now and again, very gently—you are a liar! You
are a liar!

ROBESPIERRE  My conscience is clean.

DANTON  Conscience is a mirror for a monkey to make soulful
faces at. We all dress up as best we can and go out to whatever
party we can fit into. There is no point in curling your wig if
you're not invited out. You are so delighted with your im-
maculate appearance that you will guillotine a man because he's
got a dirty shirt on. You will use his chopped-off head as a cake
of soap. The guillotine is your private washtub—you wash your
dirty linen in other people's blood. What sort of a man are you?
—You murder to defend your clean coat tails. Wait till people
spit at you, wait till they throw filth at you! Then you can defend
yourself. Not when they leave you in peace. If they are not
ashamed to run about as dirty as they are, have you the right
to stuff them in the ground? Are you the almighty police officer?
If you cannot look down on us as happily as your dear Lord
above, you'll have to hold your starchy snot-rag in front of your
face.

ROBESPIERRE  You deny virtue?

DANTON  And vice. We are all only epicures, coarse or fine. Christ
was the finest. That is the only difference among men. Every
man behaves according to his nature, he does what does him
good.—Well, Incorruptible, you've wrapped yourself up so tight
and clean—it's cruel, isn't it, to take your trousers down like
this?

ROBESPIERRE  Danton, there are times when vice is high treason.

DANTON  You dare not denounce it—that would be ungrateful—
you are too indebted to us, if only for the contrast. Even according to your prim notions, the Republic will need its models of
vice.

HÉRAULT  You'll have to create us a Committee of Public Lewdness.

LACROIX  How can *you* judge these things? You will confound the
innocent with the guilty.

ROBESPIERRE  No innocent man has ever been struck down!

DANTON  Do you hear that?—Not one innocent man! [*to* HÉRAULT
*and* LACROIX, *as they go*] We must not lose a moment. We must
declare ourselves.

ROBESPIERRE [*alone*]  Go!—He supposes that the horses of the
Revolution will pull up at the brothel, like a coachman that has
trained his nags. They will have spirit enough to drag him on
to the guillotine!—Take my trousers down! My prim notions!—
But they will say that his gigantic form cast too great a shadow
over me, that I had to drive him from the sunlight.—And if they
are right? Is it so necessary?—Yes, yes, the Republic! He must
go!—It is amusing how my thoughts spy on each other. He must
go. The ship of the Revolution shall not founder in the mud of
his shallow notions.—Away with the coterie that dresses in the
clothes of the dead aristocracy and inherits its diseases!—No
virtue! Virtue washed in the guillotine! . . . how that always
comes back to my mind . . . why can I not free my thoughts?
. . . his hand always reaching after me!—virtue wrapped up
tight and clean! . . . I may bind round myself as many rags as
I will, still the blood seeps through.—What is it in me that lies?
[*He goes to the window.*] Night snores over the earth, wallowing
in its barren dreams. Thoughts, wishes, barely imagined, di-
shevelled and shapeless, that crept away from the light of day,
now steal into the silent house of dreams. They open doors,
they stare through windows, they grow half into flesh, arms
stretched out in sleep, lips murmur—and when we are awake,
is that not a dream? Are we not sleepwalkers? Are not our actions dreams?—Who shall revile us then? In one hour the spirit
commits more deeds in thought than the lazy organism of the

body can imitate in years. Sin is in thought. Whether the body
puts it to practice is chance.

[ST. JUST *comes in.*]

ROBESPIERRE   Ha—who is there in the dark? Ah! Lights! Lights!

ST. JUST   Do you know my voice?

ROBESPIERRE   Ah, you—St. Just.

[*A servant girl brings a light.*]

ST. JUST   Were you alone?

ROBESPIERRE   Danton just left me.

ST. JUST   I met him on my way, in the Palais-Royal. He was trying
on his revolutionary face again among the rabble, surrounded
by whores, rumbling with epigrams that were whispered over
in every doorway that he passed.—We must not lose the chance
to attack. If you still hesitate, we will act without you. We are
decided.

ROBESPIERRE   What will you do?

ST. JUST   Summon the Committee of Public Safety to a special
session.

ROBESPIERRE   Very ceremonious.

ST. JUST   The distinguished corpse must be buried with respect—
by priests, not butchers—we must not mutilate it—the monster
must be buried whole.

ROBESPIERRE   Speak to the point!

ST. JUST   We shall inter him in triumph with full military honours,
and his slaves shall be slaughtered on the mound of his grave.
Lacroix—

ROBESPIERRE   Yes, a trouble-maker—go on!

ST. JUST   Hérault-Séchelles—

ROBESPIERRE   A dilettante—a handsome head!

ST. JUST   Philippeau, Camille—

ROBESPIERRE,   He too?

ST. JUST   I thought so. [*He gives* ROBESPIERRE *a newspaper.*]—
Read this.

ROBESPIERRE   Ah, he has been laughing at you, is that it? He is
a child.

ST. JUST [*pointing*]   Read this, here!

ROBESPIERRE [*reads*] "Robespierre, the Messiah of Blood, has ascended his Mount Calvary, where he sacrifices but will not be sacrificed. St. Just, who lies like John the Baptist in his bosom, prophesies to the convention the revelation of his Lord, carrying his head on his shoulders like a Holy Sacrament."

ST. JUST    I will carry his head in a basket like a potato.

ROBESPIERRE    "The genteel frockcoat of the Messiah is the winding sheet of France, his thin and twitching finger tapping on the pulpit is the blade of the guillotine."—Even you, Camille!—Have you written the denunciation?

ST. JUST    It will be easy. You prepared the brief at the Jacobin Club.

ROBESPIERRE    I wanted to frighten them.

ST. JUST    I must collect the evidence. We have a German banker, and two other foreigners accused of forgery, who can be tried with them—the charges will be conspiring with foreign governments, speculation in the currency of the Republic. . . .

ROBESPIERRE    I leave it to you!—quickly, then, tomorrow! No long death struggle! I am nervous these days. Quickly!

[ST. JUST *goes*]

ROBESPIERRE    —Messiah of Blood, who sacrifices and will not be sacrificed. He redeemed them with his blood, I redeem them with their own. He made them sin, I take the sin on myself. He had the relief of pain, I have the torment of the executioner. Who has denied himself more? He or I?—But this is trivial. Why do we always look to Him? The son of man is crucified in us all, in some Garden of Gethsemane we all wrestle in an agony of sweat and blood. But no man redeems another by his wounds. —My Camille!—They all leave me—the world is barren . . . empty—I am alone.

## Scene Six

[DANTON's *house*. DANTON *undressed, with* CAMILLE, HÉRAULT, LACROIX, *and* PHILIPPEAU, *carrying his clothes.*]

CAMILLE    Quick, Danton, we have no time to lose!

DANTON    The time loses us.—This is very tedious—we put the shirt on first, then we pull the trousers up over it, and every night we crawl into bed, and every morning we crawl out again, and we always put one foot down in front of the other. And it doesn't look as if it's ever going to be any different. It's very sad. Millions of people have already done it just the same way, and millions more are going to go on doing it—it's very sad.

CAMILLE  You are talking like a child.

DANTON  The dying are often childish.

LACROIX  Danton, you are blundering to perdition—and you will drag all your friends with you. You must cry out against the tyranny of the committee, get angry, talk of daggers and invoke Brutus—all the frightened deputies, even your enemies, the people, all Paris will join you. At least let us not die defenceless and humiliated.

DANTON  You have a bad memory. You called me a dead saint. You didn't know how right you were. I have been around to have a word with the section leaders. They were very respectful, like pallbearers. I am a relic—and relics in a revolution are thrown out as rubbish. You were right.

LACROIX  Why have you let it come to this?

DANTON  [as he is helped into his coat]  I get very bored, always finding myself wearing the same coat, and making the same creases in it! It's pitiful! To be such a poor instrument—to have only one string that plays one note—it's unbearable! . . . I wanted to make myself comfortable. I have succeeded. The Revolution has brought me peace—but not quite in the sense I meant.— Well, tell me, who do you think would support us? Our whores might fight it out with the sisters of mercy who knit by the guillotine.—The Convention—that would have been the way— but there was a month of September, when we were breaking into prisons to string up aristocrats, and we needed policemen who could keep up with us and never mind about the Convention. So we created the Committee of Public Safety outside the law. Shall we go and appeal to the Convention now? It would recognize its executioners. . . . We did not make the Revolution, the Revolution has made us. And for my part, I would rather be guillotined than guillotine. I am sick of it—we are men, why should we brawl with each other? We should sit down side by side and have peace. There was a mistake in our creation, something was left out. I don't know what it is, but I know we won't find it by pawing in each other's innards. Why do we break open our bodies? God, we are miserable medicine men!

CAMILLE  More poignantly phrased—how long shall mankind in its eternal starvation devour its own flesh? Or, how long shall we shipwrecks thirst unquenchably to suck the blood from each other's veins? Or, poor mathematicians in flesh, we strain to calculate the everlasting secret X and write our equations with the torn and bleeding limbs of our fellow men!

DANTON   You are a powerful echo.

CAMILLE   Keep me beside you. They may hear us yet.

PHILIPPEAU   Shall France be left to her executioners?

DANTON   Why not? France finds them very congenial. The people have their misery. What more can one ask, if one wants to be virtuous, and never bored? One may die of the guillotine, or the pox, or old age! But one can carry one's chains right up on to the boards, and rattle them, and exit with pretty gestures and get a bit of applause. That suits us all. We spend our lives on the stage. Only the death scene at the end is real. It's quite right that the preliminaries should be cut down a little. Our costumes are too big for us, we could never fill them out. Life ought to be an epigram—who has breath and spirit nowadays for an epic poem in fifty or sixty cantos? Some of us must drink our drop of essence in a liqueur glass—in one good mouthful—and then what?—I'll shout it to you: life isn't worth the trouble it takes to keep it going.

HÉRAULT   Then flee, Danton!

DANTON   If I could carry my country on the soles of my shoes!— Anyway, the trouble is, they wouldn't dare.—[to CAMILLE] Come on, my boy—I tell you, they wouldn't dare. Adieu, adieu!

[DANTON goes off with CAMILLE.]

PHILIPPEAU   He just walks away.

LACROIX   And doesn't believe a word he's said. Nothing but laziness! He would rather be guillotined than take himself seriously.

PHILIPPEAU   What shall we do?

HÉRAULT   Go home—and like Lucretia study a respectable end.

[They go out.]

## Scene Seven

[A promenade. CITIZENS, LADIES and GENTLEMEN, ROSALIE, MARION, a BEGGAR, a BALLAD-SINGER. SIMON and another CITIZEN.]

CITIZEN   My darling Jacqueline has . . . I mean, my virtuous Cor—. . .

SIMON   Cornelia, citizen, Cornelia!

CITIZEN  My virtuous Cornelia has blessed me with a little baby boy.

SIMON  Has born the Republic a son, citizen!

CITIZEN  Born the Republic? That sounds as if the whole—

SIMON  That thought is treason, citizen. The Republic is virtuous. The rights of the individual must yield to the rights of the people.

CITIZEN  That's what my wife says when I catch her with Louis the butcher's boy.

BEGGAR [sings]
    Love is blind
    Pleasures all mankind
    Blind is delight
    All day and all night
    The cares and the sorrows come after.

CITIZEN  My wife wants to call the baby Louis too—after the blessed saint, she says. But he was a traitor. And the boy must be an upright citizen of the Republic. Can you think of a name, citizen?

SIMON  Call him Pike, citizen.

CITIZEN  Pike! That's it! A very good name! Thank you, citizen. —Pike Robespierre Brutus Dubois.

SIMON  A revolutionary name, citizen! The breasts of your Cornelia, like the udders of the Roman she-wolf—no, that won't do, Romulus was a tyrant, that's not right.

BEGGAR [sings]
    A handful of earth and a little bit of moss . . .
    [holds out his hand to ladies and gentlemen, passing]
    Good gentlemen, lovely ladies!

FIRST GENTLEMAN  Rascal, work! You look very well nourished.

ANOTHER GENTLEMAN [giving him money]  There . . . he has a hand like satin. Shameless!

BEGGAR  Sir, how did you get your coat?

GENTLEMAN  By work! You could have the same. I will give you work. Come and see me, I live at . . .

BEGGAR  Sir, why do you work?

GENTLEMAN  Fool, to get the coat.

BEGGAR  So you work for pleasure, sir?—For a coat is a pleasure, is it not, sir? Rags would do you as well.

GENTLEMAN   Yes . . . I suppose so.

BEGGAR   You would be more virtuous, if you were an idle fool, sir. Work is a vice.—A handful of earth and a little bit of moss . . .

ROSALIE [to MARION]   Look! Here come some soldiers. I haven't had a bite since yesterday.

[Enter SOLDIERS.]

SOLDIER   Halt!—Where are you going, children?

ROSALIE [to SOLDIER]   How old are you?

SOLDIER   As old as my little finger.

ROSALIE   You're very sharp.

SOLDIER   I'll sharpen myself on you.
   [sings]
      Does he hurt you in the larder, Marianne?
      Are you crying in the larder, Marianne?

ROSALIE [sings]
      Let him try and hurt me harder, if he can,
      Or I'll wish he'd never started, little man!

[The SOLDIER and ROSALIE go off.]

[Enter DANTON and CAMILLE]

DANTON [to CAMILLE]   The whole world is on the prowl for pleasure—the smell of it is in the air, the sun is pouring down lewdness.

YOUNG GENTLEMAN   Ah, madam, the tolling of a bell, the afternoon light in the trees, the golden sunshine . . .

LADY   The scent of flowers, these natural joys, the pure pleasure of nature. Just look, Eugénie, only virtue has eyes for this.

EUGÉNIE [kisses her mother's hand]   Oh, mama! . . . I never look at anything but you.

LADY   You're a dear good child.

YOUNG GENTLEMAN [whispers to EUGÉNIE]   Look at her—the fashionable creature with the old man.

EUGÉNIE   I know her.

YOUNG GENTLEMAN   How dare she wear such a girlish hair style? Do you know what they call it? Sabine Virgin.

EUGÉNIE   Oh, you're wicked!

YOUNG GENTLEMAN  The old man is hugging himself. He thinks he's picked a budding flower—he'll take it for a walk in the sun and think he's the shower that opens it up.

EUGÉNIE  How dreadful!—I'm sure I'm blushing.

YOUNG GENTLEMAN  You're making me go pale.

DANTON [to CAMILLE]  None of your solemnity. I don't see why people don't stand still in the street and laugh in each other's faces. They ought to lean out of their windows and jump out of their graves in fits—the sky should burst, and the earth should split with laughter.

ANOTHER GENTLEMAN  I can tell you, it's the most extraordinary discovery. All our scientific techniques take on an entirely new aspect. Humanity is rushing with giant steps towards the millennium.

A SECOND GENTLEMAN  Have you seen the new play? It has the most marvellous idea in it—a Babylonian palace built on different levels, filled with people having a party—and the whole thing is blown up! The whole stage explodes! It's the symbol of our time! People faint every night. You must see it! . . . [he stops suddenly] . . . oh!

THE OTHER GENTLEMAN [taking his arm]  What's the matter?

THE SECOND GENTLEMAN  I nearly didn't see it in time—the puddle—I nearly stepped in it . . . thank you.

THE OTHER GENTLEMAN  You're not frightened?

THE SECOND GENTLEMAN  Haven't you read about it?—The earth's crust is getting thinner every year. Eventually we will all fall through. The holes may appear anywhere. We must be very careful.—But you must see the play. It's the symbol of our time!

[They go out.]


## Scene Eight

[CAMILLE'S house. CAMILLE and DANTON are talking. LUCILLE is with them.]

CAMILLE  I tell you, nothing means anything to anybody except what they see in the theatre, or a concert, or an art exhibition. Wooden copies of reality! Cut them out a puppet, so that they can see the strings that make it jump about, and make its joints creak in iambic pentameter—what a character! What significance! Take some bit of feeling, a moral, a theme, and stick a coat and trousers on it, paint its face, and let the thing torture itself through three acts until it either gets married or shoots itself—an ideal! Or fiddle out an opera full of trills and soupy tunes that sound as much like the soul of man as a penny water-whistle sounds like a nightingale—ah! Art!—Shove the people out of the theatre into the street—uh! Vulgar reality! They forget their God for his bad copyists. Creation is all around them—inside them—like a raging fire, and they take no notice. They go to the theatre, read poems and novels, practise being like the people in books, and say to God's own creatures, How ordinary! The Greeks knew what they were talking about when they said Pygmalion's statue might have come alive, but it never had any children.

DANTON   Artists play with nature like David—in September, when the murdered corpses were being thrown out of the prisons into the street, he took out his sketchbook and said, I must capture the last gasps of life in these monsters.

CAMILLE   September—the slaughter of a thousand and eighty-nine Ideals!

[HÉRAULT *enters in haste.* DANTON *goes immediately apart to talk to him.* CAMILLE *stays with* LUCILLE.]

CAMILLE   What do you say, Lucille?

LUCILLE   Nothing—I like to watch you talking.

CAMILLE   Do you listen to what I say?

LUCILLE   Of course!

CAMILLE   Am I right? Do you know what I was talking about?

LUCILLE   No—not really.

[HÉRAULT *goes.* DANTON *comes back.*]

CAMILLE   What is it?

DANTON   The Committee of Public Safety has ordered my arrest. Hérault came to let me know a hiding place.—They want my head. I'm tired of their bungling. Let them take it. I will know how to die with courage; it's easier than living. When men go smiling to the scaffold, it's time to break the scythe of death.

CAMILLE   Danton, there is still time!

DANTON   No!—but I would never have thought . . .

CAMILLE   Laziness!

DANTON   I am not lazy! I am tired! The soles of my feet burn me.

CAMILLE   Where will you go?

DANTON   Yes, who knows?

CAMILLE   Seriously, where?

DANTON   For a walk, my boy, for a walk.

[DANTON *goes out.*]

LUCILLE [*frightened*]   Oh! Camille!

CAMILLE   Be quiet, little baby.

LUCILLE [*taking hold of his head*]   When I think that they might
. . . your head! . . . Oh, my Camille, that's madness! . . . do
you think I'm going mad?

CAMILLE   Calm yourself, my darling—Danton and I are not the
same man.

LUCILLE   The world is so big, there are so many things in it—why
just this one? Why should they take it away from me? It's so
cruel—what good is it to them?

CAMILLE   Listen to me—calm yourself!—I spoke to Robespierre
yesterday. He was very friendly. It was a little strained. We have
different points of view, that's all.

LUCILLE   Go and see him now! . . .

CAMILLE   We sat on the same bench at school. He was very sombre
and lonely. I was the only one that took any trouble with him
and made him laugh. He's always been very partial to me.—I'm
going out.

LUCILLE   So soon, my darling?—go on . . . come here! . . . [*she
goes to him*] . . . just this . . . and this! [*she kisses him*] Go
on . . . go on! . . .

[CAMILLE *goes out.*]

LUCILLE   It's a dreadful time, there's nothing we can do about it.
We must just keep a firm hold on ourselves.
        Part, oh parting
        Whoever invented it?
. . . why should that come into my head? That's not very good,
for it to find its way there all by itself.—When he is out, it's as if
he might never be able to come back to me . . . as if he'd have
to go further and further away from me, always . . . The room is
so empty, the windows are all open as if we had a dead body
in the house.—I can't stay inside! . . .

[*She runs out.*]

## Scene Nine

[*An open field.* DANTON *is walking.*]

DANTON  I'll go no further. There is quietness here. Let the clattering of my footsteps and the rattling of my breath be silent.

[*He sits down.*]

Somebody once told me about a sickness that makes you lose your memory. Death ought to be like that. With any luck it might be even more serious and make you lose everything.—If only it could! . . . then why am I running away? To save my memory? Like Christ I embrace my enemy.—A safe hiding place? . . . safe for my memory, not for me. My safety is in the grave, to forget, to kill my memory.—Shall I save myself or my memory? The answer is easy.

[*He gets up and turns in the direction he came from.*]

I flirt with death. It's very pleasant, at a distance like this, to make eyes at him through one's quizzing-glass. Finally, one can only laugh at the whole business. I know that it will always be the same, tomorrow will be just like today, and the day after, and eternity will be just the same. It's a lot of noise! They want to frighten me, they wouldn't dare!

[*He goes back the way he came.*]

## Scene Ten

[DANTON's *house; night.* DANTON *walks to the window.*]

DANTON  Will it never stop? Will the lights never burn out, will the sound never die? Must we always watch and hear ourselves in our foul sins?—September!

JULIE [*from inside*]  Danton! Danton!

DANTON  Ah?

JULIE [*coming in*]  Why did you cry out?

DANTON  Did I cry?

JULIE  You spoke of foul sins, and then you groaned, September!

DANTON  I did? . . . I said nothing . . . I was hardly thinking . . . only still and secret thoughts!

JULIE  You're trembling, Danton!

DANTON  Should I not tremble, when the walls blab? When my body lets loose my thoughts to wander on my lips and speak to the stones?—it is strange!

JULIE  George, my George!

DANTON  Yes, Julie, it is strange. I will never dare to think again, if my thoughts can speak by themselves. There are thoughts, Julie, not meant for any ears . . . it is not right for them to scream at their birth like children . . . it is not right!

JULIE  God keep you in your senses!—George, George, do you know me?

DANTON  Eh? Why not?—You are a human being—and you are a woman—and you are my wife—and the earth has five continents, Europe, Asia, Africa, America, and Australia, and twice two is four. You see, I am in my right mind. Did it cry, September? Did you say that?

JULIE  Yes, Danton, through the whole house I heard it.

DANTON  As I came to the window—[*he looks out*]—the city is silent, all the lights are out.

JULIE  There's a child crying somewhere.

DANTON  As I came to the window, there was screaming and moaning in the streets—September!

JULIE  You were dreaming, Danton!

DANTON  Dreaming? Yes, I was dreaming, but that was not the dream . . . I'll tell you—my poor head is weak—yes! . . . the earth writhed beneath me and leapt out of its path. I seized it like a wild horse, I dug giant hands into its mane and squeezed its flanks. My head was wrenched sideways, my hair was streaming, I was dragged through an endless void. Then I cried out in agony and I woke up—and I walked to the window—and then I heard it, Julie.—What does that word mean? Why that word?—What have I to do with it? Why does it turn like a bloody head to *me*? I did not strike it!—Oh, help me, Julie . . . my mind is numb . . . September, Julie! . . .

JULIE  The tyrants were forty hours from Paris.

DANTON  The defences were broken, the city was full of aristocrats.

JULIE  The Republic was lost.

DANTON  Yes—lost! We could not leave the enemy at our back. we would have been fools . . . we had to . . . the stronger treads down the weaker, isn't that justice?

JULIE  Yes, yes.

DANTON  We slaughtered them—were they not guilty?—It was not murder, it was war.

JULIE  You saved France.

DANTON  I did—it was self-defence, I had to . . . The man on the Cross suffered it . . . Evil must come, but woe to him by whose hand the evil cometh—It must! Who has decreed the *must?* Who? —What is it within us that lies, whores, steals, and murders? We are puppets strung on to unknown powers—nothing, nothing ourselves! The swords that spirits fight with—we never see the hands that brandish us . . . Now I am quiet.

JULIE  Rest, my love, rest.

DANTON  Yes, Julie, come, to bed.

[*They go out.*]

## Scene Eleven

[*A* street. St. JUST *is* talking to SIMON *and some* CITIZENS *of* SIMON'S *section.*]

ST. JUST  He was as poor as you.—Now he has rich clothes, a luxurious house, he eats venison on silver dishes, he bathes in Burgundy, and has all kinds of sickly pleasures.

SIMON  Yes! He sleeps with our wives and daughters when he is drunk.

ST. JUST  Where does his money come from?—Foreigners, German bankers pay him to betray the Republic. The Duke of Orleans sends him money to buy back the throne of France!

SIMON  And send us to the guillotine.

ST. JUST  What does Robespierre take for himself?—Virtuous Robespierre, you all know him, he has nothing.

SIMON  [*with some* CITIZENS]  Long live Robespierre!

[ST. JUST *leaves them.*]

SIMON  Forward, citizens!—We answer with our heads for this. Dead or alive!—He is powerfully built.

ONE CITIZEN  He has a beautiful wife.

ANOTHER CITIZEN  Who's going to tear them apart, then?

SIMON  I will lead, citizens.—One street to Freedom!—Look after my wife. I will leave her a crown of oak leaves.

ANOTHER CITIZEN  She'll have acorns enough in her lap without your oak-leaves.

SIMON  Forward, citizens!—The honor of France! Long live the Republic!

## Scene Twelve

[*The National Convention.* LEGENDRE *and a group of moderate* DEPUTIES *are talking before the session.*]

LEGENDRE  The slaughter of deputies will never cease. Who is safe, if Danton falls?

A DEPUTY  What can we do?

ANOTHER DEPUTY  He must be tried here in the Convention before us—that will be safe enough. What will they dare to charge him with, if he can speak in his own defence before the Republic?

ANOTHER DEPUTY  Impossible!—The decree of the Committee prevents it.

LEGENDRE  The decree must be repealed, or an exception made. I will make the motion. I count on your support.

PRESIDENT  The fourteenth day of Germinal in the third year of the Republic. The Convention is declared in session.

[LEGENDRE *rises to speak.*]

LEGENDRE  Four members of the National Convention were arrested last night. I know that Danton is one of them. The names of the others are still kept secret. Whoever they may be, I demand that they be tried here before the bar of the Convention.— Citizens, I take Danton to be as honorable as myself—and I believe that no reproach can be made against me. I attack no member of the Committee of Public Safety, but I have good reason to believe that private hate and private prejudice may have been trying to deprive those men of their freedom who have rendered the Republic the greatest services of all. The man who in our darkest hour saved France by his own energy and great example deserves a hearing. He must be allowed to defend himself if he is now accused of high treason.

[*Confusion*]

SOME VOICES  We support Legendre's motion.

FIRST MODERATE DEPUTY  We are here in the name of the people —deputies may not be removed from their places without the consent of their electors.

COLLOT [*from the Committee*]  You have taken those words out of the mouths of the dead deputies of the Gironde. They reek of corpses. Is it privilege you want? The blade of the law hangs over *all* heads.

LEGENDRE  We will not allow the Committee to send our legislators to the guillotine without trial before the law.

ANOTHER MODERATE DEPUTY   We appeal to the law.

COLLOT   There is no appeal for criminals—except crowned criminals on a safe throne.

BILLAUD   Only criminals demand the right of appeal.

MODERATE DEPUTY   Only murderers do not recognise it.

ROBESPIERRE   I demand a hearing.

PRESIDENT   Will Legendre yield?

ROBESPIERRE   The confusion in this assembly has suggested for some time that a great business is in hand. The question appears to be whether a handful of men shall be allowed to defeat the will of the people.—How can you so despise your principles as to grant today to some individuals what yesterday you denied to Hébert, Dumouriez, and so many others? What is this discrimination in favor of a few men? Some deputies in this assembly lavish speeches of praise on each other. What do they mean?—these self-congratulations. The history of the Revolution has taught us very clearly what to make of the cult of particular personalities. We may not ask if a man has done this or that patriotic action; we examine his entire political life and loyalty.— Legendre appears not to know the names of the prisoners. The whole Convention knows them. His friend Lacroix is one. Why does Legendre appear not to know it? Because only shamelessness can defend Lacroix. He named only Danton, because he believes that to this name is attached some privilege.—No! We want no privileges! We want no idols!

[Cheers]

Some deputies in this assembly will try to frighten you. They will tell you that the powers that you yourselves exercise are being misused. They will cry out against "the despotism of the Committee"—as if the trust which the people have placed in you and you have vested in your Committee were not a sure guarantee of its patriotism.

Is there any deputy in this assembly who is frightened of our justice? I say to you, whoever trembles at this moment is guilty! For innocence never trembles before our vigilance.

[Great cheering]

Some people have tried to frighten me. They have told me that the danger which threatened Danton might one day threaten me. They have appealed to me, saying that some of Danton's friends were mine. Did they hope that memories of old friendship might weaken my passion for freedom? Let me say now that nothing shall make me weaken, nothing shall frighten me, even if Danton's danger shall be my own. We all have need of courage and greatness of soul. Only criminals and common souls tremble when their fellows fall from their sides. For when no crowd of accomplices surrounds them, they feel the light of truth shine full upon them. There may be some such feeble souls in this assembly. But the Republic stands by souls that are heroic. The number of cowards among us is not great—a few heads still shall fall, and France shall be saved.

[*Cheers*]

I demand that Legendre's motion be withdrawn.

St. Just   There appear to be a few sensitive ears in this assembly that cannot bear the word *blood*. A few general observations may persuade them that we are no more terrible than nature and our time. Nature calmly and irresistibly follows its laws. The man who comes into conflict with them is destroyed. A change in the composition of the air, a flare-up of the fires in the centre of the earth, a fluctuation in the poise of a mass of water, and a plague, a volcanic eruption, a flood, bury thousands of men. What is the result? An insignificant, in the larger sense quite unremarkable, change in physical nature, which would have passed unnoticed if corpses did not lie in its wake. I ask you: shall spiritual nature be more considerate in its revolutions than physical nature? Shall we not expect an idea to destroy what opposes it as well as a law of science? Shall an event take place which revolutionizes the entire shape of moral nature (I mean mankind) and shed no blood? The footsteps of mankind are slow. They can only be counted in centuries, behind each of which stretch the graves of generations. The success of our simplest discoveries and principles has annihilated some millions of human beings, who died on the way. Is it not obvious that a Revolution, where the rush of history is bold and implacable, which must accomplish in four years the achievement of a century, shall be punctuated with more fervent celebrations of slaughter? Moses led his people through the Red Sea and the wilderness until the old and decadent generation was destroyed, before he founded the new city. Legislators! We have neither the Red Sea nor the wilderness, but we have the guillotine. The Revolution dismembers mankind for its rebirth. Humanity shall rise up from the cauldron of blood in all the strength and purity of the first creation.

[*Sustained cheering. Some* Deputies *stand in their enthusiasm.*]

All the secret enemies of tyranny in Europe and throughout the world that bear under their cloaks the dagger of Brutus—we call upon them now to share this sublime moment with us!

[*The* Deputies *sing the Marseillaise.*]

# PART TWO

## Scene Thirteen

[*The Prison of the Luxembourg.* CHAUMETTE, PAINE, HÉRAULT-SÉCHELLES, *and other* PRISONERS.]

A PRISONER  Now our executioners put their necks on the block in our midst. An innocent man may not even die in the privacy of his own honesty.

HÉRAULT  Your honesty is to be thrifty and rich when the people have no bread. Why shouldn't they cut off your head? They cut off mine because it is better looking than theirs. The lava of the Revolution moulds traitors of us all. The honest men die among the thieves. In a plague no man's infection is more unjust than another's. Even a purse-proud, God-fearing parliamentarian should die for his country without reviling his fellow-traitors.

CHAUMETTE [*pulls* PAINE'S *sleeve*]  Paine . . . the fear came over me again a moment ago . . . my head aches—help me a little with your logic—I feel very dismal.

HÉRAULT [*to* PRISONER]  How can you complain of dying in bad company? That man was a priest who denied his God for the Revolution, which now will send him to the guillotine, if the pox doesn't kill him first. Poor man, he has only an English atheist to absolve him from the fear that the God he has offended may exist after all.

CHAUMETTE  Be quiet! . . . be quiet! . . . Help me, Paine.

PAINE  Come along then, philosopher of pure reason, I will give you your catechism. *There is no God*—for either God has created the world, or He hasn't. If He hasn't, the world caused itself and there is no God, for he can only be God if He is the creator of all things. But God cannot have created the world, for either creation is external like Him, or it had a beginning. In which case God must have created it at a particular moment in time. God, after resting for an eternity, must have got busy, which means He must have undergone a change in His nature and allowed the notion of time to condition Him. But that is against the very nature of God. So God cannot have created the world. The world was created by itself. So God cannot exist. *Quad erat demonstrandum.*

CHAUMETTE  Ah yes! . . . thank you! . . . that gives me light again . . . yes—thank you, thank you.

PRISONER  But what if creation is eternal?

35

CHAUMETTE    No, no—be quiet! . . .

PAINE    Then it is no longer a creation. It is an attribute of God himself. In which case God exists in all of us—in you, sir, in me, and in our philosopher here. That is not such a bad idea. But you will agree that it does not say much for the celestial majesty if within every one of us He suffers from the toothache or gets the pox. When any of us dies God is buried alive, the experience of which he must have several times a day.

CHAUMETTE    Oh, no . . . no! . . .

PAINE    Calm yourself, philosopher.

PRISONER    But creation cannot have caused itself. The creator must be a perfect being.

PAINE    It's a very human need, having to imagine God as a busy, perfect creator, just like ourselves. If we have to worship some harmonious being of serene blessedness, must we imagine Him poised over a kitchen table pounding dough to make gingerbread men? And doing it out of an eternal need for our love and sympathy? I would be happy to accept a less exalted father who did not bring his children up so far below his own station—in pigsties, and in gutters. Wish away every cause of suffering in life, and you can prove that God exists. Listen, philosopher—why do I suffer? That is the rock of atheism. The least little twinge of pain in any atom of the universe tears a hole in God's creation from top to bottom.

HÉRAULT    You are safe, philosopher. God is nought. Chaos will re-absorb you. No angry old judge will wake you up, complaining—you pulled a naked whore through the streets and worshipped her instead of me. Your goddess of reason has sentenced you to hellfire already, in the groin.

CHAUMETTE    Thank you, thank you . . . I am grateful to you, gentlemen.

PAINE    [to HÉRAULT] He still does not believe it. To make a safe end, he'll take extreme unction, turn towards Mecca, and have himself circumcised, so no way to salvation fails for want of trying.

[DANTON, PHILIPPEAU, LACROIX, and CAMILLE are led into the cell. HÉRAULT goes quickly to DANTON and embraces him.]

HÉRAULT    Good morning!—I should say good night. I can't ask you if you slept well. How will you sleep?

DANTON    Well, well, we must go laughing to bed.

LACROIX  I never thought they would strike so quickly.

DANTON  I knew. He warned me.

LACROIX  And you said nothing?

DANTON  Why? It's better to die of a stroke. Did you want to be ill beforehand?—and I didn't think they would dare. [to HÉRAULT] Anyway, it's better to lie in the earth than to let her rub corns on to your feet. I would rather use her as a cushion than a treadmill.

HÉRAULT [to LACROIX]  Would you have us grow into dirty old men that stroke pretty faces with calluses on our fingers?

CAMILLE  Why do you waggle your tongues? The cold sweat of death is on your foreheads. You'll never lick it off.—Oh, Lucille!

A PRISONER  Liberty, Equality, Fraternity, or death!

ANOTHER [to CAMILLE]  Well, Attorney General of the Lamppost, your improvements in street lighting have made France no brighter.

PAINE  Leave him alone! This is the revolutionary who first spoke the word mercy.

[He embraces CAMILLE. Others follow his example.]

CAMILLE  My friends, we have failed. I am sent to the scaffold because my eyes could still get wet at the fate of our miserable people.

PHILIPPEAU  We are like priests—we have prayed with the dying—we have been infected and die of the same disease.

LACROIX  So many people, in such misery.

PAINE  These unhappy people, their executioners, and the guillotine are nothing but our promises come true. Paris is a slaughterhouse. We have built our Revolution on foundation stones of human heads.

DANTON  You are right—We work nowadays in human flesh only. It is the curse of our time! My body is now requisitioned.—One year ago today I created the Revolutionary tribunal. I ask God and mankind for pardon. I wanted to prevent further September massacres. I hoped to save the innocent. My friends, I hoped to make it possible for you all to leave this place.

PRISONER  Oh—we will leave it!

DANTON  Now I am with you. Heaven knows how it will end.

## Scene Fourteen

[*The Revolutionary Tribunal.* ST. JUST *and* FOUQUIER-TINVILLE, JUDGE, PEOPLE, SOLDIERS.]

ST. JUST   Here are the indictments. The German bankers Freys and Westermann, and the forger Chabot, have been tried and sentenced. There was applause from the people. Charges of conspiracy linked with foreign money will be popular. Desmoulins' wife is rich and has money invested abroad. Lacroix made himself a sudden fortune in the Netherlands.

FOUQUIER   It will not be easy. Danton will frighten the jury. He is the scarecrow of the Revolution.

ST. JUST   Accuse the others first. Their defence will pass the time. Let them say what they like. Leave Danton till the third day. There will be no time left for him to upset the jury, and the charges will be gospel with the people.

FOUQUIER   [*takes list of names*]   I have had to rough-handle certain legal procedures . . .

ST. JUST   Yes?

FOUQUIER   . . . to be certain of a staunch jury.

ST. JUST   Are they reliable?

FOUQUIER   Leroi—he is deaf—Danton can shout till his throat is raw—

ST. JUST   Very good—yes?

FOUQUIER   Vilatte and Lamière—the one will be drunk, the other's an idiot. Neither ever opens his mouth except to say guilty. Renaudin—

ST. JUST   He has voted not guilty.

FOUQUIER   Only for priests. He came to me the other day in a rage and demanded that all the accused be bled before their trials to make them weaker—any noisy defendants wake him up—Leave it to me.

ST. JUST   We rely on you.

[ST. JUST *goes.* LACROIX, DESMOULINS, DANTON, HÉRAULT, *and* PHILIPPEAU *are ushered in.* LACROIX *steps into the box of the accused.*]

JUDGE   The tribunal will hear the accused.

FOUQUIER   Your name, citizen?

LACROIX   Jean Philippe Lacroix.

FOUQUIER   Your age?

LACROIX   Thirty-six.

FOUQUIER   Citizen Lacroix, you are accused of defrauding the Republic of its proper revenues during the occupation of the Netherlands, of confiscating the wages of the army of the Republic, and with the traitor Chabot of forging false currency in the name of the Republic.

LACROIX   You can sentence me to death, but I forbid you to insult me.

FOUQUIER   What have you to say in your defence?

LACROIX   Not guilty.

FOUQUIER   Your—

CAMILLE [interrupting]   Camille Desmoulins.

FOUQUIER   Your age?

CAMILLE   I am the same age as the good Jacobin Jesus of Nazareth.—A fatal age for revolutionaries.

FOUQUIER   You are accused of bribing deputies of the Convention to the allegiance of foreign powers, and, by illegal investment of a personal fortune acquired by a marriage of convenience to a woman of former royalist inheritance, of conspiring to undermine the currency of the Republic.—Have you anything to say in your defence?

[DANTON goes to the box in silence.]

FOUQUIER   Your name, citizen?

DANTON   The Revolution knows my name. My home will soon be in eternity and my name in the pantheon of history.

FOUQUIER   Danton, the Convention accuses you of conspiring with the Duke of Orleans and the faction of the so-called Louis XVII, together with foreign agents, to overthrow the government of the—

DANTON   My voice, which I have always sounded in the defence of the people, rebukes your slander. Let the miserable men who accuse me appear! And I will cover them with shame. The Committee of Public Safety must attend this judgment, I will answer only to them. I require them as accusers and as witnesses. Let them appear! You and your tribunal are nothing to me. I have told you—oblivion will soon be my refuge. My life is an appalling burden to me, you may tear it from me, I long to shake it off!

FOUQUIER  Danton, rudeness is the attribute of criminals, the innocent—

DANTON  The rudeness I have shown in fighting for my country's freedom is my most valued virtue. It is my rudeness that avails me now in the interests of the Republic against my monstrous accusers. Can I control myself in the face of so vile a slander? I am a revolutionary!—Let them expect no cold defence from me! Men of my cut are the treasure of revolutions. On our foreheads shines the aura of freedom.

[*Cries from the* PEOPLE. *The* JUDGE *rings a bell.*]

They accuse me of conspiring with foreign powers, of cringing at the feet of miserable despots. They implicate me with swindlers and convicted traitors and summon me to answer to their virtuous, inexorable justice.—You wretched St. Just, you will be responsible to the history of the world for this appalling blasphemy!

FOUQUIER  I demand that you answer your accusers calmly!

DANTON  They have laid their hands on my whole life! Let it rise and confront them! These feeble men shall be buried under the weight of my deeds for freedom!—I am not proud of my life! Destiny commands our actions, but only powerful natures are its organs. On the field of Mars I declared war on the monarchy, it was I who deposed it, and on the twenty-first of January I threw down at the feet of all the kings of Europe as the gauntlet of the besieged Republic—the head of a king!

[*The* PEOPLE *roar and cheer. The* JUDGE *rings the bell.* DANTON *grasps the indictment from* FOUQUIER'S *hand.*]

When I look at this list of platitudes and horrors, my whole being trembles! The loyalty of every citizen of the Republic is under attack! This ready-made indictment can be drawn up in mass and the names of any victim inserted to further their murderous justice! The Committee can verify no crime of which they accuse me—let my accusers appear! I am within my rights when I demand it. I shall unmask the pitiful monsters and hurl them into the oblivion from which they should never have crept!

JUDGE  Do you hear this bell?

DANTON  The voice of a man defending his honor and his life shall drown your little bell!

[*The* JUDGE *leaves the tribunal.* DANTON *speaks to the* PEOPLE.]

In September I nourished the frail bride of the Revolutio[
the bodies of slaughtered aristocrats. The gold of the mo[
was forged by my voice into the weapons of the people. M[ ~~~~
was the organ which buried the satellites of despotism under a
wave of bayonets!

[*Violent response from the* CROWD]

FOUQUIER [*to the* SOLDIERS]   Clear the crowd!

[*The* PEOPLE *are forced out of the tribunal.*]

Danton, your voice is silenced. You are too violently moved.
You shall continue your defence at the second hearing. The
tribunal is adjourned.

DANTON   Now you know your Danton—in a few hours he will rest
in the arms of fame.

[FOUQUIER *goes out.*]

LACROIX   Well roared, Danton! If you had bothered about your
life a little earlier, we would be in a different place now!

## Scene Fifteen

[*A small cell in the Luxembourg.* GENERAL DILLON, *dozing;* CITI-
ZEN LAFLOTTE, *awake. The* GAOLER, *very young, enters, carrying two bottles.*]

LAFLOTTE [*indicating* DILLON]   Ssh!

[*The* GAOLER *goes on tiptoe up to* DILLON.]

DILLON   Ssh!—You drunken rabble! The smell of you woke me up
halfway down the corridor! Ha! Ha! Ha!

[*He roars with laughter. He takes his bottle from the* GAOLER.]

LAFLOTTE   His nose lights up like a beacon at the approach of cognac. Ha! Ha! Ha!

[*He imitates* DILLON's *laughter. The* GAOLER *gives* LAFLOTTE *his
bottle and gets a tip. He takes a letter out of his pocket.*]

GAOLER   Does it give enough light to read by?

DILLON   What's that letter? Give it to me!

[*The* GAOLER *holds the letter.*]

GAOLER  Do you conspire against the people, your Excellency, or do you conspire for their good?

DILLON  Give it to me! That letter concerns the safety of the Republic!

[*The* GENERAL *finally fishes out a coin.*]

GAOLER  Ah, you conspire for the good of the people, your Excellency.

DILLON [*snatching letter*]  Be off—drunken rabble!

[*The* GAOLER *goes.*]

[*reads*]—"Danton has terrified the tribunal. The jury is wavering, and people cry for Danton against the Committee. The crowd for the second hearing stretches from the Palais de Justice across the bridge to the other side of the Seine. A handful of money, an officer to lead us—" . . . hm! . . .

[*He walks up and down, pulling at his bottle.* LAFLOTTE *watches.*]

If I could get one foot into the street!—I wouldn't let myself be slaughtered . . . yes!—One foot into the street!—

LAFLOTTE  And on to the tumbril.

DILLON  You think so! A few steps further and we might fill you a tumbril full of the corpses of the Committee. It is time! The right-minded people must lift up their heads.

LAFLOTTE [*aside*]  All the easier to chop them off. On, old man, a few more swallows, and I am afloat.

DILLON  The fools, the scum!—Lay hands on Danton! They will get themselves guillotined in the end.

[*He paces up and down.*]

LAFLOTTE [*aside*]  He must be sacrificed, then. What is it to me if I tread on a corpse as I climb out of my grave?

DILLON  One foot in the street! I will find people enough, cashiered soldiers, Girondins, ex-noblemen, we will break open the prisons, we will come to an understanding with the prisoners.

LAFLOTTE [*aside*]  It smells a bit villainous—to be an informer. But why not? I must try another angle on life, I have been too one-sided. It will give my conscience something new to sniff at—it's not nice, never changing one's smell.

DILLON  I'll write a note to Danton's wife.

[*He starts to write.*]

LAFLOTTE [*aside*]  I'm not really resigned enough to die. I might fall in love with life all over again, if I had given it to myself. You don't often get the chance to take your fate incestuously in your arms and be your own father. Who would be an Oedipus, if a man could father himself?

[DILLON *mumbles as he writes.*]

Oedipus was a fool to put out his eyes. I shall have need of mine—to weep for the poor general.

DILLON  "Who is safe if Danton falls?" . . . They swamp the rabble with corpses. Danton's and Camille's wives shall throw money to them. That will be more popular than heads.

LAFLOTTE  And the view out to the guillotine has become very boring.—To wait so long for it! I have gone through it twenty times in my imagination. I've lost all interest in it now. The whole idea seems very ordinary.

[DILLON *writes.*]

I'm not afraid of dying—only of pain. How do they know it doesn't hurt? They say it's over in a moment. But pain has a sense of time all its own. It might want to make itself felt a little longer.—No! Pain is the only sin, suffering the only vice. I must not lose my virtue.

DILLON [*the letter finished, rolls it up*]  Here Laflotte, where is the rabble? Call him—I have some money, and my plan is ready. We must strike while the iron is hot!

LAFLOTTE  We will not lose a moment, General. I'll talk to the gaoler. You can rely on me; we will get out of this hole—[*aside*] —and into another one—I to the world at large, you to a narrow grave.

## Scene Sixteen

[*The Committee of Public Safety.* ST. JUST, COLLOT D'HERBOIS, BILLAUD-VARENNES, *and* BARÈRE. *Also* FOUQUIER-TINVILLE.]

FOUQUIER  I have closed the tribunal. The outcry goes on. The Committee must appear. They have appealed to the people that they are denied witnesses, they will give no evidence except to the Committee. Their demands are repeated all over Paris. The people cheer. Danton parodies Jupiter and shakes his locks.

BILLAUD  All the easier for the executioner to get hold of them.

BARÈRE We dare not show ourselves. The fishwives and rag-pickers might find us less impressive.

COLLOT The rabble have an instinct for being downtrodden, even by looks. That sort of insolent physiognomy delights them. Danton's forehead is more arrogant than a coat of arms. The people ought to recognise by now the heads that must be severed.

BARÈRE What does Robespierre say?

ST. JUST He has locked himself in his house.

FOUQUIER If the mob is not kept out of the last hearing, we shall find ourselves on trial, with Danton pointing the finger at *us*.

ST. JUST The jury must declare itself sufficiently instructed and close the trial.

BARÈRE It's against the law.—We've let the people know that law.

ST. JUST They must go! Decadents! They are diseased! "Dare, dare, and dare again!" Danton shall not have taught us in vain. If he survives, he will have the Republic back against the wall. And he has appetite enough to ravish freedom from every one of us.

[*An* ORDERLY *enters with* LAFLOTTE.]

ORDERLY Insurrection is reported in the prisons. Citizen Laflotte has made the denunciation. General Dillon is conspiring to escape from the Luxembourg and raise an army to break up the Convention.

[BARÈRE *laughs.*]

COLLOT How was the conspiracy discovered?

ORDERLY Citizen Laflotte was in the same cell. Dillon got drunk and blabbed.

BARÈRE He's cut his own head off with a bottle.

LAFLOTTE He has written to the wives of Danton and Camille Desmoulins to distribute money among the people. Danton is to be released from the tribunal and the Committee placed under arrest.

BARÈRE Fairy tales.

ST. JUST Fairy tales with which we shall send Danton and his friends to sleep. The city is in revolt! I shall make a report before the Convention.

BARÈRE Go on, St. Just. Spin your perfect sentences—every comma the blade of the knife and every stop a chopped-off head.

St. Just  The Convention shall decree that the trial of Danton must proceed without further testimony. Any aspersion of evidence by the accused shall be declared in contempt of the tribunal.

Barère  You have the revolutionary instinct. That sounds convincingly like law and it might work too. They won't be able to keep still. Danton must roar.

St. Just [to Fouquier]  Reopen the Tribunal.

[Fouquier goes. The Orderly and Laflotte follow.]

I count on your support. There are people in the Convention who are as sick as Danton, and who fear the same cure. They have taken courage again, and will try to shout down the violation of legal forms.

Collot [bathetically passionate]  Go, St. Just! The lava of the Revolution shall flow! The sickly ravishers who would infect the womb of freedom shall be grappled to her bosom and smothered in her embrace. Go, St. Just, we strengthen your arms as you dash the thunderbolt at the heads of the cowards!

[St. Just goes.]

Barère  Sickly ravishers! The guillotine is now a prescription for the pox. We are running a hospital. Disease is against the law.

Billaud  Some of us enjoy good health.

Collot  How is your mistress?—When do you visit Clichy again?

Barère  When the doctor stops visiting me.

[The Orderly enters and places papers before Collot.]

Orderly  In St. Pélagie prisoners are dying. They ask for a doctor.

Billaud  Unnecessary. The executioners are complaining of overwork.

Orderly  There are pregnant women among them.

Collot  Their children will need no coffins.

Barère  Consumption in an aristocrat spares the tribunal a sitting. Medical aid would be counter-revolutionary.

Collot [taking one of the papers]  A personal petition to me! It's a woman.

Barère  One that wants to be forced to choose between the hard boards of the guillotine and the bed of a Jacobin. Like Lucretia she will die after the loss of her honor, but not immediately—of childbirth, or malnutrition, or senile decay. Will you inspect her virtue in the name of the Republic?

COLLOT  She is too old. Madame demands execution. She says that prison lies as heavy on her as the lid of a coffin. For four weeks she has wished only for death. The answer is easy. [*dictates to* BILLAUD] "Ancient citizeness, you have not wished for death quite long enough."

[BILLAUD *writes the answer and hands it to the* ORDERLY, *who goes out.*]

BARÈRE  Clever and virtuous! But Collot, is it a good idea to give the guillotine a sense of humor? The people will not put themselves under a doctor they can't take seriously.

BILLAUD [*counting names on a list*] . . . forty-two, forty-three, forty-four, forty-five.—Here is the list for tomorrow.

[*He hands a list to* COLLOT. *They go out.*]

BARÈRE [*alone*]  Monsters!—"You have not waited for death quite long enough!" Those words should have split the tongue that spoke them!—And I?—In a revolution, when murderers raid the prisons, the victim who would not be sacrificed joins in with the murderers—he takes a penknife out of his pocket, he sticks it in the breast of a priest, his life is saved.—He has served the Republic. Who will denounce him?—Join a mob of murderers or sit on the Committee of Public Safety—save yourself by penknife or guillotine—you must murder somebody . . . and then you must murder somebody else . . . where does it end? . . . count the barleycorns—one, two makes a pair, three, four, five makes a pile . . . come along, my conscience—chook, chook, chook!—eat them up! . . . [*squawks like a hen*] . . . don't squawk, little conscience—eat them up . . . [*squawks more contentedly*] . . . —and if I carried no knife in my pocket?—I would never have joined the murderers—I would have been dead.—[*squawks loudly*]—come along, little conscience, we must get on together as best we can.

## Scene Seventeen

[*The Revolutionary Tribunal.* DANTON, CAMILLE, HÉRAULT, LACROIX, *and* PHILIPPEAU, *waiting for the reopening of the trial.*]

LACROIX  Ah!—To have to hang about and wait for death, to watch him go through all the motions, when you know that finally he'll come right up to you with the same old nasty nod!

CAMILLE  If it was only an honest rape, and you could wrestle and sweat a little while he had his way! But with these fake formalities, it's like getting married to an old woman—you sign your name, the shameful witnesses are called in, someone says Amen, and finally the bed clothes are pulled back and in she creeps to give you her slow cold hug.

DANTON  If it were a fight! If there were something to grip or tear with your teeth! I feel as if I've fallen into a mill—slowly, scientifically, the cold machine wrenches your body apart.—To be killed so mechanically!

CAMILLE  And then to lie in the earth—who knows how long we lie and rot before death can torment the life out of our flesh?—cold, stiff, and alone in the feeling of our own decay.

PHILIPPEAU  Be calm, my friends. We shall be like autumn leaves that fall to seed at the first sign of winter. Before we live again, we must smell a bit rotten. Is that so bad?

DANTON  An elevating point of view! Reincarnation from one dung-heap to another. A scholarly theory of life and death. I've had enough of the school bench. My buttocks are as callused as a monkey's.

PHILIPPEAU  What do you hope for?

DANTON  Peace.

PHILIPPEAU  That is in God.

DANTON  In nothingness. What can you lie down in more restful than that? If God is the ultimate peace, then God must be the great void. But I am an atheist—the cursed sentence, something cannot become nothing. And I am something, that's the trouble. Creation is so richly constructed, there is no emptiness in it—a great and endless business! The void has murdered itself, the creation is its wound, we are its drops of blood, the world is its grave where it rots. That sounds crazy, but there is something true about it.

HÉRAULT  Why should we hope for release in death?—The world is the eternal creditor, it turns up everywhere when you can't pay. We would escape into nothingness, but they won't let us. The debts are always there, even if we don't pay them.

DANTON  We spend our lifetimes buried alive—like kings we have three or four coffins, one inside the other—the sky, our house, our clothes. We scratch for fifty years on the bottom of the lid. It helps to hope for annihilation in the end. But there is no hope in death, it is only a simpler, less organized form of corruption than life. That is the only difference. But I have got used to this sort of decay; the devil knows how I shall get on in the other.—

Oh, Julie . . . if I could go alone! If she would let me be so lonely . . . but if I could decay altogether, if I could dissolve, I would still be a handful of tortured dust, every atom of me could find peace only in her.—No! I cannot die! I cannot die! We are not beaten—we still cry out—they must tear every drop of life out of our bodies!

LACROIX  We must stick to our demands!—The Committee must appear as our witnesses before the tribunal!

[*Outside the tribunal.* FOUQUIER *and* ST. JUST.]

FOUQUIER  The tribunal has broken down completely. As soon as the gallery was opened, Danton burst out in a direct appeal to the people to overflow the Committee.

ST. JUST  This will stop him.

FOUQUIER  If it's in time!

ST. JUST  Suspend the trial! Danton has condemned himself— Go! Let us be rid of him!

[*Inside the tribunal.* JUDGE, SOLDIERS, CROWD.]

DANTON  The Republic is in danger! We are governed by fraud. We appeal to the people! My voice is still strong enough to halt the tumbrils of the Committee.—I repeat—we demand a commission, we shall give our evidence before the nation. We shall fortify ourselves in the garrison of reason, the cannon of truth shall burst forth, and the enemies of the people shall be destroyed!

[*Roar from the* CROWD. FOUQUIER *rushes in.*]

FOUQUIER  In the name of the Republic! Respect for the law!— the Convention decrees: insurrection is discovered in the prisons, whereby the wives of Danton and Desmoulins shall distribute money among the people, enabling the former General Dillon to escape from prison and place himself at the head of an army of traitors as the means to release the accused by armed force. The tribunal is empowered to suspend from testimony any accused who rudely or in contempt of the law shall interrupt the process of justice. The jury shall declare itself sufficiently instructed, and sentence shall be passed.

DANTON  I call upon those present—have the accused spoken in contempt of this tribunal, of the people, or its Convention?

CROWD  No! No!

CAMILLE  The wretches! They will murder my Lucille!

DANTON   One day you will know the truth. This is dictatorship!—
They have torn off the veil, they carry their heads high, they
tread upon our corpses. I accuse Robespierre, St. Just, and their
executioners of high treason. They will stifle the Republic in
blood. The tracks of our tumbrils shall be the highway of in-
vading armies into the heart of France. You want bread and
they throw you our heads—you thirst, and they make you lick
our blood from the steps of the guillotine!

[*Outcry from the* CROWD.]

THE CROWD   Long live Danton! The Committee to the guillotine!
To arms! Freedom for the Republic!

[DANTON *is removed by force from the tribunal.*]

## Scene Eighteen

[*A street.* JULIE *and a* BOY.]

JULIE   It is over. They have trembled before him. They kill him out
of fear.—Go—I have seen him for the last time—tell him, I will
not look upon him now.

[*She cuts a lock of her hair.*]

There—give him that, and say to him, he shall not go alone. He
will understand me, come quickly back, I will read his answer in
your eyes.

[*The* BOY *goes.*]

Oh, my husband! . . . shall I never see you any more? . . . my life's
beloved . . .

## Scene Nineteen

[*A cell in the Conciergerie.* LACROIX *and* HÉRAULT *huddled together.*
DANTON *and* CAMILLE, *together.*]

LACROIX   One's hair grows shabby—and one's nails—I appall myself. [*He sneezes.*]

HÉRAULT [*sits up*]   Ah!—be careful where you sneeze! You blow
dust in my eyes.

LACROIX   You kick me in your sleep, dear friend, and I have corns
on my feet.

HÉRAULT  I sleep like a lamb—it's the rats biting your toes:

LACROIX  Ah! . . . Just to be free of lice . . .

HÉRAULT  You will! Sleep well! We must see if we can't get on a little better, since there is no room to quarrel.—Just try not to scratch me when you have bad dreams—[LACROIX *turns over*]—and don't take all the blanket, it's cold!

[*They huddle together to go to sleep.*]

DANTON  Yes. Camille—tomorrow we shall be worn-out shoes tossed in the lap of that old beggar-woman, our mother earth.

CAMILLE  The leather that Plato says the angels cut their slippers from when they tread upon the earth.—My Lucille!

DANTON  Be calm, my boy!

CAMILLE  Can I? Do you think so, Danton? Can I? They cannot lay their hands on her!—The light of beauty that pours out of her sweet body can never be snuffed out. The earth would not dare to bury her, it would lift itself in an arch above her, the dew would glisten on her eyelids and bathe her arms in sleep sooner than do her harm.

DANTON  Sleep, my boy, sleep.

CAMILLE  Listen, Danton, between ourselves it is so miserable to have to die. I will steal the last pretty look from the face of life. I will keep my eyes open.

DANTON  They will stay open without your wishing it. The guillotine does not close your eyes for you. Sleep is more merciful. Sleep, my boy, sleep.

CAMILLE  Lucille, your kisses make dreams upon my lips—oh, close my eyes, and let me hold you in my arms.

DANTON  [*to his watch*]  Can you not rest, my friend?—With every tick the walls push closer in on me till they are as narrow as a coffin.—I read a story about that as a child, it made my hair stand on end.—As a child! . . . all the trouble to fatten me up and keep me warm—more work for the grave digger!—I feel as if my breath is rattling already.—My dear body, I will imagine you are a lady's salon that smells of the sweat of love and dancing and whisper pretty things to you. We have passed the time together. Tomorrow you will be a broken fiddle—the tune is played out. Tomorrow you will be an empty bottle—the wine is drunk up, and I will go sober to bed.—some happy people can still get drunk.—Tomorrow you will be the trousers that drop for the last time—you will be thrown in the bottom of the wardrobe, and the moths will eat you, and you can smell as much as you like.—Ah! that doesn't help . . . yes . . . it is miserable to have to die. Death apes birth; we die as helpless and naked as new-born babies. We were wrapped in a winding sheet for swaddling clothes—Camille! . . . asleep . . . [*he bends over him*] . . . may his dreams press gently on his eyelids and bring him peace.

[*He gets up and goes to the window.*]

I will not go alone—I thank you, Julie. But if only I could have died simply, as a star falls—as a sound breathes its last, seeming to die of its own kiss—as a ray of light drowns itself in clear water.—The stars trickle upon the sky of night like tears . . . Oh, the grief in the great eye that lets them fall! . . .

CAMILLE   Oh! . . .

[*He stands up and stretches up to the ceiling.*]

DANTON   What is it, Camille?

CAMILLE   Oh!—oh! . . .

DANTON   Are you trying to tear down the ceiling?

CAMILLE   Ah!—you . . . you!—oh, hold me!—speak to me!

DANTON   Camille!

CAMILLE   It's you that I'm—ah! . . . that is my hand—yes, I know who I am . . . ah, Danton, it was horrible! . . .

DANTON   What was it?

CAMILLE   The ceiling flew away, and the moon fell down upon me, close to me, I held it in my arms. The roof of heaven with all its lights sank down, I knocked upon it with my hand—I had the stars in my fingers—I stumbled along, I was drunk, and heaven was a sheet of ice—it was horrible! . . .

DANTON   The light makes a circle on the ceiling—that's all it was.

CAMILLE   It would take so little to make me lose my senses. Mad-ness gripped me by the hair.—I must not sleep, I must not go mad.

[*He takes a book.*]

DANTON   Do you want to read a book on your way to the grave? I'll dream of whores. I won't slink out of life as if it were a confessional. Life is a whore. Leave her lying in bed. She does her dirty business with all the world.

[*He goes to sleep.* CAMILLE *reads, wrapped in a blanket.* LUCILLE *comes outside the prison window.*]

LUCILLE  Camille! Camille!

[CAMILLE *goes to the window*.]

LUCILLE  Listen, Camille—you make me laugh in your black robe
—why do you hold that iron mask before your face? Can't you
bend down? Where are your arms?—I'll make you come home,
my bird—[*sings*]
> There are two stars in heaven
> Brighter than the moon
> One shines in my love's window
> The other in my heart

Come on, my love—softly, up the ladder—they're all asleep.
The moon has been helping me wait for you. But you can't come
in like that. Your clothes are too shabby. It's not funny any
more, you must stop it. Why don't you move? Why don't you
speak to me? You're frightening me!—Listen, people say that you
must die. And they make such solemn faces. Die! I have to laugh
at their faces. Die—what sort of a word is that? Tell me, Camille—
die—I'll think it over . . . there it is—there! I'll run after it.
Come, my darling one, help me to catch it. Come on! . . . Come
on!

[*She runs away*.]

CAMILLE  Lucille!—Lucille!

[*Morning*]

CAMILLE [*aside*]  Madness sitting behind her eyes—someone else
has gone mad—it's the way the world is—what can we do about
it? We wash our hands . . .

DANTON  I leave chaos behind me. Not one of them understands
the business of government. They might still make something of
it if I left St. Just my digestion and Robespierre my whore.

LACROIX  If they had let us live, we would have made freedom a
whore!

DANTON  She is that already. Freedom and a whore are the most
cosmopolitan things under the sun. She is now going to prosti-
tute herself respectably in a marriage-bed with an impotent
Robespierre. But she will play Clytemnestra with him. Let him
have six months' bliss. I will pull him after me.

CAMILLE [*aside*]  Heaven help her to some comforting obsession!
The notions we call sanity are all too painful to bear. The happi-
est man is the one who believes he is God the Father, the Son,
and the Holy Ghost.

LACROIX  Robespierre is a Nero. He was more friendly to Camille in the days before the arrest than ever before.—Isn't that true, Camille?

CAMILLE  What does it matter?—[aside] What a pretty thing she has made of her madness . . . why must I go now? We could have laughed with it, and rocked and kissed it.

LACROIX  The asses will cry "Long live the Republic!" when we ride by.

DANTON  Let the deluge of the Revolution wash our corpses where it will. The people will preserve our bones to knock the heads of tyrants for ever more.

HÉRAULT  The world is littered with the jawbones of asses. It is the Samsons to swing them that may be missing.

DANTON  When history opens its vaults, despotism will choke everlastingly at the smell of our corpses.

HÉRAULT  We smelled a bit strong in our lifetime too.—Your words will sound better in the mouths of posterity, Danton. They are not very sweet to us.

CAMILLE  He is setting his face as if he expected to turn to stone and be dug up by posterity as a museum piece. Must we go on pulling faces, laying on the rouge, speaking with a careful accent? . . . in the end we must make our exit into a hall of mirrors and see that we have all been playing the same decrepit and ragged toothless fool. We are our own audience. Any one can be devil, angel, idiot, or genius. We play them all no better than the next man, they are not such fat parts as we thought.—Sleep, digest, make children—that is our performance. Doing it standing on your toes doesn't make it look any prettier. We have all stuffed our faces at the same table and we all have terrible pains in our bellies—why hold up the serviette? Scream and groan? That's what we need to do. We are fellowmen. Must we try to act like noble heroes just to spare ourselves a little sympathy?

HÉRAULT  Yes, Camille, we'll sit down together and howl. It's stupid to grit your teeth when something hurts you. Greeks and gods cry out—let the Romans and stoics keep their lips pursed.

DANTON  The one was as good an epicure as the other. They all did what gave them comfort.

PHILIPPEAU  My friends, there is one ear in which the painful clamour that we raise is united in a stream of harmony.

DANTON  But we are the poor musicians, and our bodies the pitiful instruments. Does the playing of our tuneless agony sound in the distance like a sigh of delight to the almighty ear?

HÉRAULT  So we are little pigs kept for exquisite gods and whipped squealing to death to be served up as tastier flesh on high.

CAMILLE  We are lonely children that play in the light of day, only to be lost in everlasting dark, where spirits shriek eternally, and the trembling children die eternally, and the spirits rejoice at our trembling.

DANTON  The world is chaos. The great void is our only common ancestor.

[*The* GAOLER *enters. The* PRISONERS *embrace each other.*]

HÉRAULT  Be cheerful, Camille. Let us shake off our mortality carelessly and be as like the gods as we can. We shall walk up Mount Olympus in a warm and sunny afternoon.

[DANTON, CAMILLE, HÉRAULT, *and* LACROIX *go out.* PHILIPPEAU *is kept back by the* GAOLER, *and is left alone.*]

PHILIPPEAU  Good night, my friends—good night! Let us pull the blanket quietly over our heads under which all heartbeats rest and all eyes close in peace.


## Scene Twenty

[DANTON'S *house.* JULIE, *at the window.*]

JULIE  The people were running in the streets—now everything is still . . . I will not make him wait for me.

[*She takes a phial.*]

Come, beloved priest—your Amen shall send me to a blessed sleep. It is so sweet to take farewell—I have only to close the door behind me.

[*She drinks.*]

I might stand like this forever.—the sun is down, the world was so tormented in its glare, now her face looks still and solemn, like someone dying . . . how softly the sunset glows upon her forehead—paler and paler she floats upon a bed of golden air.— Is there no hand behind the clouds of time to lift her from the storm and close her eyes in peace? . . . I will leave her alone— no kiss, no touch, no sigh to wake her from her slumber— . . . Sleep! . . . sleep . . .

[*She dies.*]

## Scene Twenty-one

[*The Place de la Guillotine.* CROWD, WOMEN, CHILDREN, GUARDS, TWO EXECUTIONERS, HÉRAULT, DANTON, CAMILLE, DESMOULINS, LACROIX, LUCILLE.]

WOMAN [*with* CHILDREN]   Give me room! Give me room! My children are hungry, they scream for food. Let them see and be quiet. Give me room!

SECOND WOMAN   Hérault! He's a lovely man!

THIRD WOMAN   When I saw him marching in the parade on Constitution Day, I thought, how handsome he would look standing by the guillotine. It was second sight.

FOURTH WOMAN   You always learn something, watching people dying.

[*The* PRISONERS *sing the Marseillaise.*]

FOURTH WOMAN   Hey, Danton! Now you can do it with the worms.

SECOND WOMAN   Hérault! Leave me your pretty hair for a wig!

HÉRAULT   Cut some of the hair off your face!

CAMILLE   Hags! Who will cry mercy for you now?

THIRD WOMAN   Cry mercy for yourself!

DANTON [*to* CAMILLE]   Calm, my boy, you have shouted yourself hoarse.

CAMILLE [*giving a coin to the* EXECUTIONER]   There's for the waiter! —My friends, I will serve myself first. We will have a classical supper. We will lie down at our places and pour a little blood for grace.—Adieu, Danton!

[*He embraces* DANTON, *ascends the platform, and is guillotined.* LACROIX *follows.*]

LACROIX [*to the* CROWD]   You kill us on the day that you have lost your reason. You will kill them the day you get it back again.

HÉRAULT [*to* DANTON]   I wonder will he pull out his shirt and show them all he has clean linen.

[LACROIX *is guillotined.*]

HÉRAULT   Oh . . . Danton—I can't think of anything funny to say. It's time.

[HÉRAULT *starts to embrace* DANTON. *The* EXECUTIONER *pulls him away on to the platform.* DANTON *stops the* EXECUTIONER.]

DANTON  Would you be more terrible than death? You can't keep our heads from kissing at the bottom of the basket.

[HÉRAULT *is executed.* DANTON *follows him. The bodies of the executed and the basket of heads are wheeled away, followed by the* CROWD, *who sing the Marseillaise. The* EXECUTIONERS *remain to clean the guillotine.* LUCILLE, *alone.*]

LUCILLE  . . . it's something very serious . . . I must think—I'm beginning to understand it—die? . . . die! . . . but everything is allowed to live, everything—every fly and little bird . . . why not him?—The whole world moves, the bells are clanging, the people are running, and water is running—everything is going on and on—it mustn't! No!—I will lie on the ground and scream and everything will be frightened, and the world will stop dead and never move again.

[*She gets down on the ground, and covers her face with her hands, and lets out a cry. In a moment she gets up.*]

It didn't help—everything is the same as it was—the houses, the street . . . the wind still blows, the clouds still pass us by. We must put up with it.—My Camille! Where shall I look for you now?

FIRST EXECUTIONER [*finishing his work*]
    And when I stroll home,
    The moon shines so bright—
Hey! You nearly finished?

SECOND EXECUTIONER  In a minute!
    —My father he stands at the window.
    My boy, you have been in a fight!

FIRST EXECUTIONER  Throw me my jacket!

[*They go off singing.* LUCILLE *sits on the steps of the gillotine.*]

LUCILLE  I will sit in your lap—silent angel of death.
[*sings*] Death is God's reaper.
    All men must sing.
    And women must weep—oh.
You lovely cradle that rocked my Camille to sleep, and stopped his breath with red roses. You soft-tongued funeral bell, that sang sweet songs to him, and laid him in the earth.

[*sings*] The scythe makes us sleepers.
     All men must sing.
     And women must weep—oh.

[*A* WATCH-PATROL *of* CITIZENS *passes.*]

CITIZEN   Who is there?

LUCILLE [*remembering, then as if making a decision, suddenly*]
    Long live the king!

CITIZEN   In the name of the Republic!

[*She is surrounded by the* PATROL *and led away.*]

THE END